POPE FRANCIS

A Stranger and You Welcomed Me

POPE FRANCIS

A Stranger and You Welcomed Me

A Call to Mercy and Solidarity
with Migrants and Refugees

Edited by Robert Ellsberg

ORBIS BOOKS

Maryknoll, New York 10545

Founded in 1970, Orbis Books endeavors to publish works that enlighten the mind, nourish the spirit, and challenge the conscience. The publishing arm of the Maryknoll Fathers and Brothers, Orbis seeks to explore the global dimensions of the Christian faith and mission, to invite dialogue with diverse cultures and religious traditions, and to serve the cause of reconciliation and peace. The books published reflect the views of their authors and do not represent the official position of the Maryknoll Society. To learn more about Maryknoll and Orbis Books, please visit our website at www.maryknollsociety.org.

Library of Congress Cataloging-in-Publication Data

Names: Francis, Pope, 1936– author. | Ellsberg, Robert, 1955– editor.
Title: A stranger and you welcomed me : a call to mercy and solidarity with migrants and refugees / Pope Francis ; edited by Robert Ellsberg.
Description: Maryknoll : Orbis Books, 2018.
Identifiers: LCCN 2018016372 (print) | LCCN 2018029409 (ebook) | ISBN 9781608337699 (e-book) | ISBN 9781626983038 (pbk.)
Subjects: LCSH: Emigration and immigration—Religious aspects—Catholic Church. | Church work with immigrants—Catholic Church. | Church work with refugees. | Immigrants. | Refugees. | Church work—Catholic Church. | Catholic Church—Doctrines.
Classification: LCC BX1795.E44 (ebook) | LCC BX1795.E44 F7313 2018 (print) | DDC 261.8/328—dc23
LC record available at https://lccn.loc.gov/2018016372

"Think of the Holy Family,
Our Lady, St. Joseph, and the Child Jesus,
who fled to Egypt to escape violence
and to find refuge among strangers.
Remember too the words of Jesus:
'Blessed are the merciful,
for they shall obtain mercy' (Mt 5:7).
Take these words with you always,
so that they can bring you encouragement and consolation."

—*Address to Members of the Jesuit Refugee Service, November 14, 2015*

"Solidarity, this word that frightens the developed world.
People try to avoid saying it.
Solidarity to them is almost a bad word.
But it is our word!
Serving means recognizing and accepting
requests for justice and hope and seeking roads together,
real paths that lead to liberation."

—*Visit to the Jesuit Refugee Service in Rome, September 10, 2013*

"A person who thinks only about building walls,
wherever they may be, and not building bridges,
is not Christian.
This is not the gospel."

—*Pope Francis, speaking to reporters on a flight from Mexico to Rome,*
February 17, 2016

Contents

Foreword by Cardinal Joseph W. Tobin, C.Ss.R.   xiii

Introduction by Robert Ellsberg   xvii

PART I
ADDRESSES, HOMILIES, AND PRAYERS

"Where Is Your Brother?"   3
Homily on the Island of Lampedusa, July 8, 2013

No One Is a Stranger   8
Address to Participants in the Plenary
of the Pontifical Council for the Pastoral Care
of Migrants and Itinerant People, May 24, 2013

Serving, Accompanying, Defending   12
Visit to the Jesuit Refugee Service in Rome,
September 10, 2013

The Flight into Egypt   17
Angelus, Saint Peter's Square
Feast of the Holy Family of Nazareth, December 29, 2013

"Come to Me" 19

Angelus, St. Peter's Square, July 6, 2014

The Church Is with You 21

Greeting to Young Refugees Assisted by the Salesians,
Cathedral of the Holy Spirit, Istanbul,
November 30, 2014

A United Response 23

From an Address to the European Parliament,
Strasbourg, France, November 25, 2014

With Jesus at the Center 24

Address to the Federation of Christian
Organizations for International Volunteer Service,
December 4, 2014

A Throwaway Culture 26

Address to Members of the Diplomatic Corps
Accredited to the Holy See, January 12, 2015

Prayers for Migrants 29

A Land of Dreams 32

Remarks from the Pope's Visit to the United States,
September 2015

A Tragic Exodus 35

Address to Members of the Jesuit Refugee Service,
November 14, 2015

Humanity on the Move   38
   Address to Members of the Diplomatic Corps
   Accredited to the Holy See, January 11, 2016

Crossing Borders   45
   Homily in Ciudad Juárez, Mexico, February 17, 2016

Do Not Lose Hope!   48
   Mòria Refugee Camp, Lesbos, Greece, April 16, 2016

Solidarity and Mercy   50
   Address to Members of the European Confederation
   and of the World Union of Jesuit Alumni and Alumnae,
   September 17, 2016

"A Stranger and You Welcomed Me"   53
   General Audience, St. Peter's Square, October 26, 2016

Migrants Are Persons   57
   Address to Members of the Diplomatic Corps
   Accredited to the Holy See, January 9, 2017

Justice, Civility, and Solidarity   60
   Address to Participants in the International Forum
   on "Migration and Peace," February 21, 2017

A Pilgrim People   68
   Address to the National Directors of Pastoral Care
   for Migrants of the Catholic Bishops' Conferences
   of Europe, September 22, 2017

Loving the Other, the Stranger, as Ourselves   72
   Homily for World Day of Migrants and Refugees,
   Vatican Basilica, January 14, 2018

A Merciful Gaze   75
   Meeting with the Sant'Egidio Community
   on the Fiftieth Anniversary of Its Foundation,
   March 11, 2018

Ideologies Striking at the Heart of the Gospel   79
   From the Apostolic Exhortation
   Gaudate et Exsultate *(Nos. 100–103),*
   March 19, 2018

Migrants and Refugees:
Men and Women in Search of Peace   82
   Message for the Celebration of the Fifty-first
   World Day of Peace, January 1, 2018

PART II
MESSAGES FOR THE WORLD DAY OF
MIGRANTS AND REFUGEES

Message for 2014   93
Migrants and Refugees: Toward a Better World

Message for 2015   100
Church without Frontiers, Mother to All

Message for 2016 105
Migrants and Refugees Challenge Us:
The Response of the Gospel of Mercy

Message for 2017 111
Child Migrants, the Vulnerable, and the Voiceless

Message for 2018 118
Welcoming, Protecting, Promoting,
and Integrating Migrants and Refugees

Final Words 126
> *From a Message for the Second Holy See–Mexico*
> *Conference on International Migration*
> *June 14, 2018*

Foreword

By Cardinal Joseph W. Tobin, C.Ss.R.

I am grateful for the invitation to comment on *A Stranger and You Welcomed Me: The Call to Mercy and Solidarity with Migrants and Refugees*. This collection presents homilies, addresses, and commentaries of Pope Francis on the great drama of our times, a modern Passion Play whose actors are refugees and migrants, the Church, and the world. Pope Francis points out just what is at stake for each of the three groups. Refugees and migrants risk losing their lives. The rest of us could lose our souls.

Pope Francis is thoroughly convinced of both threats. Since his election in March 2013, he has given unmistakable priority to justice for a significant portion of the global community. The 2017 *International Migration Report* of the United Nations estimated that there are now 258 million people living in a country other than their country of birth—an increase of 49 percent since 2000. The number of refugees, asylum-seekers, and internally displaced people around the world has topped 65 million.

The Holy Father, however, rarely recites statistics. He insists on restoring the human faces of those who have been

reduced to numbers or brutalized by vile epithets. Reading
his words, you will be impressed by his constant effort to remind the world that migrants and refugees are human beings, our brothers and sisters, children of God—not simply
"illegals," or "aliens," or "enemy combatants," or "the worst
of the worst." He never tires of directing us to the words of
Jesus: that the anxious face of the apparent "stranger" is the
muddied, bloodied visage of the Lord.

Pope Francis is concerned about our faces as well, faces
that are marred by indifference, greed, distraction, and a
craving for novelty that blinds us to our brothers and sisters.
Faces that one day will sputter, "When did we see you a
stranger and not welcome you?" Francis begs that we learn
the answer now, before it is too late. We may choose to reject
the gospel message, but we cannot pretend that God's word
does not summon us to recognize their faces, our faces, His
Face.

Lately I have wondered about the rising number of sui-
cides among the people of the most affluent nation on earth.
Where did their hope go? Despite the incredible perils that
refugees and migrants accept in their journey, they are
driven by hope to flee places of death and destruction.
Speaking of migrants during his visit to the United States in
2015, Pope Francis told the bishops of this country, "The
Church in the United States knows like few others the hopes
present in the hearts of these 'pilgrims.'" Failure to recognize and respond to hope hardens our hearts and disfigures
our faces. Can hearts that have been armored against the
hopes of the "other" spot the hopelessness of the most vulnerable among us?

The Holy Father insists that our response of love to Jesus'
love of us, and our willingness to share that love with others,

form the most important reality in our lives, and not just when we are doing something "religious." He has warned us against "the gray pragmatism of the daily life of the Church, in which all appears to proceed normally, while in reality faith is wearing down and degenerating into small-mindedness" (*Joy of the Gospel*, 83).

This good pope invites us to recover the magnanimity symbolized by a green-clad "parishioner" of the archdiocese I serve: the Lady in the harbor who holds high a torch so that "huddled masses yearning to breathe free," the "homeless," and the "tempest-tossed" can find a golden door. The spirit of that Lady represents the United States at its best. Pope Francis spoke to that spirit during his visit in 2015: "Do not be afraid to welcome them. Offer them the warmth of the love of Christ and you will unlock the mystery of their heart. I am certain that, as so often in the past, these people will enrich America and its church."

Introduction

By Robert Ellsberg

Pope Francis established his concern for the plight of migrants and refugees on his very first trip outside of Rome, just months after his election as pope. On the Italian island of Lampedusa, a waystation for many refugees making their way to Europe, he celebrated Mass and commemorated the thousands who have died at sea. Their fate, he said, confronts us with the same question that God put to Cain: "Where is your brother?" It was an occasion for the pope to introduce one of his signature concerns: the "globalization of indifference" that makes it difficult for us even to recognize our brothers and sisters. "The culture of comfort, which makes us think only of ourselves, makes us insensitive to the cries of other people, makes us live in soap bubbles which, however lovely, are insubstantial...We have become used to the suffering of others: it doesn't affect me; it doesn't concern me; it's none of my business!"

And so for the pope the issue is not only the plight of defenseless people, forced to contend with heartless traffickers and the perils of a journey that has made of the Mediterranean Sea "a vast cemetery," and whose blood cries out to

God. It is fundamentally a question that God puts to the rest of us, especially Christians: Where are we? Who are we? The tears of migrants and refugees find a damning counterpart in our own lack of tears: "Has any one of us wept because of this situation and others like it? . . . Today has anyone wept in our world?"

That is a question that underlies the homilies, speeches, prayers, and documents collected in this volume. The pope does not offer colorful stories or memorable anecdotes. He does not assemble facts or statistics, nor does he set out to propose specific policies or measures for reform. His aim is to awaken a spirit of mercy and solidarity, in hopes that such a spirit will inspire whatever response we make—whether as individuals, as communities, or as nations. He proposes, in essence, a single simple message repeated in a hundred different ways: migrants and refugees are human beings, precious in the eyes of God; they are our brothers and sisters; they are worthy of respect; what we do for them, we do directly for Christ.

Does such a simple message require a whole book? One might as well ask Pope Francis why he finds it necessary to repeat this message on so many occasions and in so many ways. Over and over, he returns to this theme, whether he is visiting refugee camps in the Middle East, or preaching at the Mexican border town of Ciudad Juarez, or speaking to a joint session of the U.S. Congress (where he reminded his audience that he too, was the son of immigrants). It is the subject of his annual messages for the World Day of Migrants and Refugees, each of them focused on a different aspect of the problem. He even introduced the subject into his recent apostolic exhortation on the call to holiness, *Gaudate et Exsultate*: "We often hear it said that, with respect to relativism and the flaws of our present world, the situation of migrants, for example, is a lesser issue. Some Catholics consider it a secondary issue compared to the 'grave' bioethical questions. That a politician looking for votes might say such a thing is understandable, but not a Christian, for whom the only proper attitude is to stand in the shoes of those brothers and sisters of ours who risk their lives to offer a future to their children."

Repeatedly, he anchors his concern in simple texts from scripture: the repeated commandment to "welcome the stranger" and the reminder that "you yourselves were strangers in the land of Egypt" (Ex 22:21); the words of Jesus, "I was a stranger and you welcomed me" (Matt 25:36); and above all, the reminder that the Holy Family themselves, in their flight into Egypt, shared the experience of contemporary refugees.

Clearly, for Pope Francis, our response to the challenge posed by migrants and refugees is not simply another political or economic problem, but a profound test of Christian faith. As he notes in his apostolic enhortation on holiness,

> If I encounter a person sleeping outdoors on a cold night, I can view him or her as an annoyance, an idler, an obstacle in my path, a troubling sight, a problem for politicians to sort out, or even a piece of refuse cluttering a public space. Or I can respond with faith and charity, and see in this person a human being with a dignity identical to my own, a creature infinitely loved by the Father, an image of God, a brother or sister redeemed by Jesus Christ. That is what it is to be a Christian! Can holiness somehow be understood apart from this lively

recognition of the dignity of each human being? (*Gaudate et Exsultate*, 98)

The problem of mass migration, of course, involves the many motivating factors—social, economic, and political— that cause so many individuals and families to leave their homes and undertake the perilous journey to a new land. Among these are dire poverty, political or religious persecution, the impact of climate change, ethnic cleansing, war and violence in many forms. ("At times they leave not so much in search of a better future, but any future at all, since remaining at home can mean certain death.") On the other side, their arrival on the borders or coastlines of new countries imposes its own social, economic, and political challenges. The pope is not indifferent to these problems. But he bids us not to be guided primarily by fear and resentment of the "other." In setting public policy it makes all the difference if we begin with the acknowledgment of migrants and refugees as fellow human beings, infinitely loved by God, as opposed to "refuse cluttering a public space."

Certainly, the pope's words are directed at a global audience. He has not generally addressed specific debates in the United States. (A notable exception occurred during an inflight exchange with reporters in 2016, when he was asked about candidate Donald Trump's promise to build a wall on the Mexican border: "A person who thinks only about building walls, wherever they may be, and not building bridges, is not Christian. This is not the gospel.") Nevertheless, if the pope regards the issue of migrants and refugees as a defining item in his agenda, he has apparently found his opposite counterpart in the current president of the United States.

Donald J. Trump literally inaugurated his presidential campaign in June 2015 with a press conference in Trump Tower in which he assailed the impact of Mexican immigrants: "When Mexico sends its people, they're not sending their best. They're not sending *you* ... They're sending people that have lots of problems ... They're bringing drugs. They're bringing crime. They're rapists. And some, I assume, are good people." The supposed dangers posed by "illegal aliens" inspired the promise of his campaign mantra to "build the wall." Following his election he canceled the Deferred Action for Child Arrivals program (DACA), which has provided protections to hundreds of thousands of young people who came to this country as children; he has taken measures to expel hundreds of thousands of refugees from Haiti and Central America, here for decades under provisions for victims of natural disasters. (The president reportedly asked why we take so many people from "s**thole countries" instead of places like "Norway.") Such measures were not based on actual threats posed by people who had been obeying the law, working, paying taxes, and contributing to their communities for many years. He has consistently blurred the lines between immigrants in general and violent gang members whom he delights in calling "animals." Most controversially, his administration implemented a policy of separating children—even infants and toddlers—from their parents when they were apprehended at the border. In the face of legal challenge and public outrage, this policy was rescinded—yet uncertainty continues.

At the same time, immediately upon his election the president tried to fulfill a campaign promise to impose "a complete and total shutdown of Muslims entering the United States until our country's representatives can figure out what the hell is going on." At first stymied by lower courts, this policy, in a cosmetically adjusted form, was eventually upheld by the Supreme Court. The administration has been successful in reducing the admission of refugees to the United States by over 70 percent.

Quite apart from humanitarian considerations, the question has been raised of whether such policies contradict the longstanding image of the United States—a nation essentially formed by waves of immigrants—as a beacon of freedom and opportunity. The Statue of Liberty, after all, bears the famous poem by Emma Lazarus:

> Give me your tired, your poor,
> Your huddled masses yearning to breathe free,
> The wretched refuse of your teeming shore.
> Send these, the homeless, tempest-tost to me,
> I lift my lamp beside the golden door!

In response, Stephen Miller, the president's chief advisor on immigration policy, observed, "I don't want to get off into a whole thing about history here, but the Statue of Liberty is a symbol of American liberty lighting the world. The poem that you're referring to was added later and is not actually part of the original Statue of Liberty." So there.

Yet in his speech to Congress in 2015—long before this issue had reached a boiling point—Pope Francis spoke of America as a land of dreams, "dreams which awaken what is deepest and truest in the life of a people." He spoke specifically of the "millions of people who came to this land to pursue their dream of building a future of freedom." As the son of immigrants, he pointed out that so many of those in his audience (if not all of them), were also descended from immigrants. "For those peoples and their nations, from the heart of American democracy," he said, "I wish to reaffirm my highest esteem and appreciation." While acknowledging that many of these original immigrants encountered hostility and violent opposition, nonetheless, he insisted, "when the stranger in our midst appeals to us, we must not repeat the sins and the errors of the past ... Building a nation calls us to recognize that we must constantly relate to others, rejecting a mindset of hostility in order to adopt one of reciprocal subsidiarity, in a constant effort to do our best. I am confident that we can do this."

From a distance of three years the pope's appeal to the golden rule ("to treat others with the same passion and compassion as we would like to be treated") and his confidence in the capacity of Americans to embrace the better angels of their history may seem blissfully naïve. With each passing week, official policies and accompanying rhetoric seem to set new standards in heartlessness and division, as if explicit denial of the pope's call for mercy and solidarity were the prerequisite for Making America Great Again. Even those who call themselves Christians are not immune to these divisive siren calls. A recent survey showed, in fact, that among all segments of American society white Evangelical Christians are the group most likely to express hostility toward migrants and refugees. Such attitudes, of course, are not unique to the United States. The pope's words are equally directed and equally challenging to audiences in Italy, Germany, and the rest of Europe. As he observes, "Many destination countries have seen the spread of rhetoric decrying the risks posed to national security or the high cost of welcoming new arrivals, and thus demeaning the human dignity due to all as sons and daughters of God. Those who, for what may be political reasons, foment fear of migrants instead of building peace are sowing violence, racial discrimination, and xenophobia, which are matters of great concern for all those concerned for the safety of every human being."

Who knows whether any hearts and minds will be changed by the pope's oft-repeated message? Nevertheless, he urges us to consider that it is not only migrants and refugees who are the victims of our hard-heartedness. Those of us who turn a blind eye, who tell ourselves, "It doesn't concern me; it's none of my business!" are also the losers. As he notes, "The poor are also the privileged teachers of our knowledge of God; their frailty and simplicity unmask our selfishness, our false security, our claim to be self-sufficient. The poor guide us to experience God's closeness and tenderness, to receive his love in our life, his mercy as the Father who cares for us, for all of us, with discretion and with patient trust."

The title of this volume, "A Stranger and You Welcomed Me," is taken from Jesus' reminder that it is he who walks among us in the form of the poor and needy. "I was hungry and you fed me; I was thirty, and you gave me a drink; I was a stranger and you welcomed me . . . Insofar as you did these things for the least of my brothers and sisters, you did them for me." Our very salvation is tied to this test. But it is the following verse, and the fate of those who fall short, that should resound in our ears: "Insofar as you failed to do these things for one of these, however humble, you did not do them for me."

If, in this "culture of comfort," we have lost our bearings, it may be the stranger among us who is calling us home.

PART I

ADDRESSES, HOMILIES, AND PRAYERS

"Lord, in this liturgy, a penitential liturgy, we beg forgiveness for our indifference to so many of our brothers and sisters. Father, we ask your pardon for those who are complacent and closed amid comforts that have deadened their hearts; we beg your forgiveness for those who by their decisions on the global level have created situations that lead to these tragedies. Forgive us, Lord!"

—Homily on the Island of Lampedusa, July 8, 2013

"Where Is Your Brother?"

Homily on the Island of Lampedusa
July 8, 2013

(Note: In his first trip outside Rome, following his election, Pope Francis traveled to the Italian island of Lampedusa, a major point of entry for refugees making their way to Europe. There he celebrated Mass to commemorate the thousands who have perished along the way, particularly those who have drowned in the Mediterranean Sea.)

Immigrants dying at sea, in boats that were vehicles of hope and became vehicles of death. That is how the headlines put it. Since I first heard of this tragedy a few weeks ago, and realized that it happens all too frequently, it has constantly come back to me like a painful thorn in my heart. So I felt that I had to come here today, to pray and to offer a sign of my closeness, but also to challenge our consciences lest this tragedy be repeated. Please, let it not be repeated! . . .

This morning, in the light of God's word that has just been proclaimed, I wish to offer some thoughts meant to challenge people's consciences and lead them to reflection and a concrete change of heart.

"Adam, where are you?" This is the first question God asks man after his sin. "Adam, where are you?" Adam had lost his bearings, his place in creation, because he thought he could be powerful, able to control everything, be God. Harmony was lost; man erred, and this error occurs over and over again also in relationships with others. "The other" is no longer a brother or sister to be loved, but simply someone who disturbs my life and my comfort.

God asks a second question: "Cain, where is your brother?" The illusion of being powerful, of being as great as God, even of being God himself, leads to a whole series of errors, a chain of death, even to the spilling of a brother's blood!

God's two questions echo even today, as forcefully as ever. How many of us, myself included, have lost our bearings! We are no longer attentive to the world in which we live; we don't care; we don't protect what God created for everyone—and we end up unable even to care for one another! And when humanity as a whole loses its bearings, the result is tragedies like the one we have witnessed.

"Where is your brother?" His blood cries out to me, says the Lord. The question is not directed to others; it is a question directed to me, to you, to each of us. These brothers and sisters of ours were trying to escape difficult situations, to find some serenity and peace; they were looking for a better place for themselves and their families, but instead they found death. How often do such people fail to find understanding, fail to find acceptance, fail to find solidarity? And their cry rises up to God! Once again I thank you, the people of Lampedusa, for your solidarity. I recently listened to one of these brothers of ours. Before arriving here, he and the others were at the mercy of traffickers, people who exploit the poverty of others, people who live off the misery of others. How much these people have suffered! Some of them never made it here.

"Where is your brother?" Who is responsible for this blood? In Spanish literature we have a comedy of Lope de Vega which tells of how the people in the town of Fuente Ovejuna kill their governor because he is a tyrant. They do it in such a way that no one knows who the actual killer is. So, when the royal judge asks: "Who killed the governor?" they all reply: "*Fuente Ovejuna*, sir." Everybody and nobody!

Today too, the question has to be asked: Who is responsible for the blood of these brothers and sisters of ours? Nobody! That is our answer. It isn't I; I don't have anything to do with it; it must be someone else, but it is certainly not I. Yet God is asking each of us: "Where is the blood of your brother which cries out to me?" Today no one in our world feels responsible. We have lost a sense of responsibility for our brothers and sisters. We have fallen into the hypocrisy of the priest and the Levite whom Jesus described in the parable of the Good Samaritan: we see our brother half dead on the side of the road and perhaps we say to ourselves, "Poor soul...!" and then we go on our way. It's not our responsibility, we think, and and with that we feel reassured, assuaged.

The culture of comfort, which makes us think only of ourselves, makes us insensitive to the cries of other people, makes us live in soap bubbles which, however lovely, are insubstantial; they offer a fleeting and empty illusion that results in indifference to others; indeed, it even leads to the globalization of indifference. In this globalized world, we have fallen into globalized indifference. We have become used to the suffering of others: it doesn't affect me; it doesn't concern me; it's none of my business!

Here we can think of the character called "the Unnamed" in Alessandro Manzoni's novel. The globalization of indifference makes us all "unnamed"—responsible, yet nameless and faceless.

"Adam, where are you?" "Where is your brother?" These are the two questions that God asks at the dawn of human history, that he also asks each man and woman in our own day, and that he also asks us. But I would like us to ask a third question: "Has any one of us wept because of this situation and others like it?" Has any one of us grieved for the death of these brothers and sisters? Has any one of us wept for these persons who were on the boat? For the young mothers carrying their babies? For the men who were looking for a means of supporting their families? We are a society that has forgotten how to weep, how to experience compassion— "suffering with" others. The globalization of indifference has taken from us the ability to weep! In the Gospel we have heard the crying, the wailing, the great lamentation: "Rachel weeps for her children...because they are no more." Herod sowed death to protect his own comfort, his own soap bubble. And so it continues...

Let us ask the Lord to remove the part of Herod that lurks in our hearts. Let us ask the Lord for the grace to weep over our indifference, to weep over the cruelty of our world, of our own hearts, and of all those who in anonymity make social and economic decisions that open the door to tragic situations like this. "Has any one wept?" Today has anyone wept in our world?

Lord, in this liturgy, a penitential liturgy, we beg forgiveness for our indifference to so many of our brothers and sisters. Father, we ask your pardon for those who are complacent and closed amid comforts that have deadened their hearts; we beg your forgiveness for those who by their decisions on the global level have created situations that lead to these tragedies. Forgive us, Lord!

Today too, Lord, we hear you asking: "Adam, where are you?" "Where is the blood of your brother?"

No One Is a Stranger

Address to Participants in the Plenary of the Pontifical Council
for the Pastoral Care of Migrants and Itinerant People
May 24, 2013

Dear brothers and sisters,

The "trade in people" is a vile activity, a disgrace to our societies, which claim to be civilized! Exploiters and clients at all levels should make a serious examination of conscience both in their own hearts and before God! Today the Church is renewing her urgent appeal that the dignity and centrality of every individual always be safeguarded with respect for fundamental rights, as her social teaching emphasizes. She asks that these rights be extended to the millions of men and women on every continent whose rights are not recognized. In a world in which much is said about rights, how often is human dignity actually trampled upon! In a world in which so much is said about rights, it seems that the only thing that has any rights is money. Dear brothers and sisters, we are living in a world where money rules. We are living in a world, in a culture where the fixation on money holds sway.

You have rightly taken to heart the situations in which the family of nations is called to intervene, in a spirit of fraternal solidarity, with programs of protection, often against a background of dramatic events that affect the lives of so many people almost every day. I express my appreciation and gratitude, and I encourage you to continue on the path of service to the poorest and most marginalized of your brothers and sisters.

Let us remember Paul VI's words: "For the Catholic Church, no one is a stranger, no one is excluded, no one is far away" (Homily for the Closing of the Second Vatican Council, December 8, 1965). Indeed, we are a single human family that is journeying toward unity, making the most of solidarity and dialogue among peoples living in a world of diversity and differences.

The Church is a mother, and her motherly attention is expressed with special tenderness and closeness to those who are obliged to flee their own country and exist between rootlessness and integration. This tension destroys people. Christian compassion—"suffering with," compassion—is expressed first of all in the commitment to learning about the events that force people to leave their homelands, and, where necessary, to give voice to those who cannot manage to make their cry of distress and oppression heard. By doing this you also carry out an important task in sensitizing Christian communities to the multitudes of their brethren scarred by wounds that mark their existence: violence, abuse, distance from family love, traumatic events, flight from home, uncertainty about the future in refugee camps. These are all dehumanizing elements and must spur every Christian and the whole community to practical concern.

Today, however, dear friends, I would like to ask you all to see a ray of hope as well in the eyes and hearts of refugees and of those who have been forcibly displaced—a hope that is expressed in expectations for the future, in the desire for friendship, in the wish to participate in the host society through learning the language, access to employment, and the education of children. I admire the courage of those who hope to be able gradually to resume a normal life, waiting for joy and love to return to brighten their existence. We can and must all nourish this hope!

Above all I ask leaders and legislators and the entire international community to confront the reality of those who have been displaced by force with effective projects and new approaches in order to protect their dignity, to improve the quality of their lives and to face the challenges that are emerging from modern forms of persecution, oppression, and slavery.

They are human people—and I stress this—who are appealing for solidarity and assistance, who need urgent action but also and above all understanding and kindness. God is good, let us imitate God. Their condition cannot leave us indifferent. Moreover, as Church we should remember that in tending the wounds of refugees, evacuees, and the victims of trafficking, we are putting into practice the commandment of love that Jesus bequeathed to us when he identified with the foreigner, with those who are suffering, with all the innocent victims of violence and exploitation. We should reread more often chapter 25 of the Gospel according to Matthew in which he speaks of the Last Judgment (cf. vv. 31–46). And here I would also like to remind you of the attention that every pastor and Christian community must pay to the journey of faith of Christian refugees and Christians uprooted from their situations by force, as well as of Christian emigrants. These people need special pastoral care that respects their traditions and accompanies them to harmonious integration into the ecclesial situations in which they find themselves. May our Christian communities really be places of hospitality, listening, and communion!

Dear friends, let us not forget the flesh of Christ, which is in the flesh of refugees: their flesh is the flesh of Christ. It is also your task to direct all the institutions working in the area of forced migration to new forms of co-responsibility. This phenomenon is unfortunately constantly spreading. Hence your task is increasingly demanding in order to promote tangible responses of closeness, journeying with people, taking into account the different local backgrounds.

Upon each one of you I invoke the motherly protection of Mary Most Holy, that she may illuminate your study and your action. For my part, I assure you of my prayers, my closeness, and also my admiration for all that you are doing in this area. I bless you warmly. Many thanks.

Serving, Accompanying, Defending

Visit to the Jesuit Refugee Service in Rome
September 10, 2013

Dear brothers and sisters, Good afternoon!

I first greet all of you refugees. Thank you for your powerful, heart-rending stories. Each one of you, dear friends, has a life story that speaks to us of the tragedies of war, of conflicts that are all too often linked to international politics. Yet, above all, every one of you bears a wealth of humanity and a religious sense, treasures to welcome rather than to fear. Many of you are Muslim or members of another religion. You come from various countries, from different situations. We mustn't be afraid of differences! Brotherhood enables us to discover that they are riches, gifts for everyone! Let us live in brotherhood!

Rome! For many people our city is the second stage on the journey, after Lampedusa and the other places to which they arrive. Often, as we have heard, the journey they make is hard. It is grueling and even violent—I am thinking especially of the women, of the mothers who bear all of this to assure for their children a future and the hope of a different life for themselves and their families. Rome should be the city that makes it possible for them to rediscover a human dimension and to begin to smile again. How often, however, as in other areas, many people here who have "international protection" stamped on their residency permits are forced to live in distressing situations—at times degrading—and in no way are they able to start living a dignified life or to think of a new future! . . .

It is lovely that Christian men and women as well as people who belong to other religions and even non-believers are working for the refugees alongside the Jesuits, united in the name of the common good, which for us Christians is above all love of the Father in Christ Jesus. *Serving, accompanying, defending:* three words that constitute the program of work for the Jesuits and their co-workers.

The first word: *Serving.* What does this mean? Serving means giving an attentive welcome to a person who arrives. It means bending over those in need and stretching out a hand to them, without calculation, without fear, but with tenderness and understanding, just as Jesus knelt to wash the apostles' feet. Serving means working beside the neediest of people, establishing with them first and foremost human relationships of closeness and bonds of solidarity. Solidarity, this word that frightens the developed world. People try to avoid saying it. Solidarity to them is almost a bad word. But it is our word! Serving means recognizing and accepting requests for justice and hope, and seeking roads together, real paths that lead to liberation.

The poor are also the privileged teachers of our knowledge of God; their frailty and simplicity unmask our selfishness, our false security, our claim to be self-sufficient. The poor guide us to experience God's closeness and tenderness, to receive his love in our life, his mercy as the Father who cares for us, for all of us, with discretion and with patient trust.

From this place of welcome, encounter, and service, I would therefore like to propose that everyone, all the people who live here, in this diocese of Rome, ask themselves: Do I bend down over someone in difficulty or am I afraid of getting my hands dirty? Am I closed in on myself, on my possessions, or am I aware of those in need of help? Do I serve only myself or am I able to serve others, like Christ who came to serve even to the point of giving up his life? Do I look in the eye those who are asking for justice, or do I turn my gaze aside to avoid looking them in the eye?

The second word: *Accompanying*. In recent years the Astalli Center has grown. At the outset it offered services of basic hospitality: a soup kitchen, a place to sleep, legal assistance. It expanded to accompany people in their search for a job and efforts to fit into society. Then it also proposed activities that would contribute to building a culture of acceptance, a culture of encounter and of solidarity, starting with the safeguarding of human rights.

Accompanying on its own is not enough. It is not enough to offer someone a sandwich without at the same time making the effort to help that person learn how to stand on his or her own two feet. Charity that leaves the poor person as he is is not sufficient. True mercy, the mercy God gives to us and teaches us, demands justice; it demands that the poor find a way to be poor no longer. It asks—and it asks us, the Church, us, the city of Rome—it asks the institutions—to ensure that no one ever again stand in need of a soup-kitchen, of makeshift-lodgings, of legal assistance in order to have his or her legitimate right to live and to work, to be fully a person, recognized. Adam said: "It is our duty as refugees to do our best to be integrated in Italy." And this is a right: integration! And Carol said: "Syrians in Europe feel the great responsibility not to be a burden. We want to feel we are an active part of a new society." This too is a right! This responsibility is the ethical basis, it is the power to build together. I wonder: Do we accompany people in this process?

The third word: *Defending*. Serving and accompanying also means defending, it means taking the side of the weakest. How often do we raise our voice to defend our own rights but are indifferent to the rights of others! How many times we either don't know or don't want to give voice to the voice of those—like you—who have suffered and are suffering, of those who have seen their own rights trampled upon, of those who have experienced so much violence that it has even stifled their desire to have justice done!

It is important for the whole Church that welcoming the poor and promoting justice not be entrusted solely to "experts" but be a focus of all pastoral care, of the formation of future priests and religious, and of the ordinary work of all parishes, movements, and ecclesial groups. In particular—this is important and I say it from my heart—I would also like to ask religious institutes to interpret seriously and with responsibility this sign of the times. The Lord calls us to live with greater courage and generous hospitality in communities, in houses, and in empty convents. Dear men and women religious, your empty convents are not useful to the Church if they are turned into hotels and earn money. The empty convents do not belong to you; they are for the flesh of Christ, which is what refugees are. The Lord calls us to live with greater courage and generosity, and to accept them into our communities, houses, and empty convents. This of course is not something simple; it requires our acceptance of responsibility, but also requires courage. We do a great deal, but perhaps we are called to do more, firmly accepting and sharing with those whom Providence has given us to serve, overcoming the temptation of spiritual worldliness to be close to simple people and, especially, to the lowliest. We need communities with a spirit of solidarity that really put love into practice!

Every day, here and at other centers, so many people, mainly young people, stand in line to get a hot meal. These people remind us of the sufferings of humanity. But that queue also tells us to do something, right now, everyone. It is possible. It is enough to respond to the knock at the door and to try to say: "Here I am. How can I give you a hand?"

The Flight into Egypt

Angelus, Saint Peter's Square
Feast of the Holy Family of Nazareth, December 29, 2013

Dear Brothers and Sisters,

Good morning!

On this first Sunday after Christmas, the liturgy invites us to celebrate the Feast of the Holy Family of Nazareth. Indeed, every nativity scene shows us Jesus together with Our Lady and St. Joseph in the grotto of Bethlehem. God wanted to be born into a human family, he wanted to have a mother and father like us.

And today the Gospel presents the Holy Family to us on the sorrowful road of exile, seeking refuge in Egypt. Joseph, Mary, and Jesus experienced the tragic fate of refugees, which is marked by fear, uncertainty and unease (cf. Mt 2:13–15; 19–23). Unfortunately, in our own time, millions of families can identify with this sad reality. Almost every day the television and newspapers carry news of refugees fleeing from hunger, war, and other grave dangers in search of security and a dignified life for themselves and for their families.

In distant lands, even when they find work, refugees and immigrants do not always find a true welcome, respect, and

17

appreciation for the values they bring. Their legitimate expectations collide with complex and difficult situations that at times seem insurmountable. Therefore, as we fix our gaze on the Holy Family of Nazareth as they were forced to become refugees, let us think of the tragedy of those migrants and refugees who are victims of rejection and exploitation, who are victims of human trafficking and of slave labor. But let us also think of the other "exiles": I would call them "hidden exiles," those exiles who can be found within their own families: the elderly, for example, who are sometimes treated as a burdensome presence. I often think that a good indicator for knowing how a family is doing is seeing how their children and elderly are treated.

Jesus wanted to belong to a family that experienced these hardships, so that no one would ever feel excluded from the loving closeness of God. The flight into Egypt caused by Herod's threat shows us that God is present where people are in danger, where they are suffering, where they are fleeing, where they experience rejection and abandonment; but God is also present where people dream, where they hope to return in freedom to their homelands and plan and choose life for their families and dignity for themselves and their loved ones.

"Come to Me"

Angelus, St. Peter's Square, July 6, 2014

Dear Brothers and Sisters

Good morning!

In this Sunday's Gospel, we find Jesus' invitation: "Come to me, all who labor and are heavy laden, and I will give you rest" (Mt 11:28). When Jesus says this, he has before him the people he meets every day on the streets of Galilee: very many simple people, the poor, the sick, sinners, those who are marginalized...These people always followed him to hear his word—a word that gave hope! Jesus' words always give hope!—even just to touch the hem of his garment. Jesus himself sought out these tired, worn-out crowds like sheep without a shepherd (cf. Mt 9:35–36), and he sought them out to proclaim to them the Kingdom of God and to heal many of them in body and spirit. Now he calls them all to himself: "Come to me," and he promises them relief and rest.

This invitation of Jesus reaches to our day and extends to the many brothers and sisters oppressed by life's precarious conditions, by existential and difficult situations that at times lack valid points of reference. In the poorest countries, but also on the outskirts of the richest countries, there are so many weary people, worn out under the unbearable weight of neglect and indifference. Indifference: human indifference causes the needy so much pain! And worse is the indifference of Christians! On the fringes of society so many men and women are tried by indigence, but also by dissatisfaction with life and by frustration. So many are forced to emigrate from their homelands, risking their lives. Many more, every day, carry the weight of an economic system that exploits human beings, imposing on them an unbearable "yoke" that the few privileged do not want to bear. To each of these children of the Father in heaven, Jesus repeats: "Come to me, all of you." But he also says it to those who have everything, but whose heart is empty and without God. Even to them, Jesus addresses this invitation: "Come to me." Jesus' invitation is for everyone, but especially for those who suffer the most.

Jesus promises to give rest to everyone, yet he also gives us an invitation that is like a commandment: "Take my yoke upon you, and learn from me; for I am gentle and lowly in heart" (Mt 11:29). The "yoke" of the Lord consists in taking on the burden of others with fraternal love. Once Christ's comfort and rest are received, we are called in turn to become rest and comfort for our brothers and sisters, with a docile and humble attitude, in imitation of the Teacher. Docility and humility of heart help us not only to take on the burden of others but also to keep our personal views, our judgments, our criticism, or our indifference from weighing on them.

Let us invoke Mary Most Holy, who welcomes under her mantle all the tired and worn-out people, so that through an enlightened faith, witnessed in life, we can offer relief for so many in need of help, of tenderness, of hope.

The Church Is with You

Greeting to Young Refugees Assisted by the Salesians
Cathedral of the Holy Spirit, Istanbul
November 30, 2014

Dear Young People,

I have greatly desired to meet with you, youth from Turkey, Syria, Iraq, and other countries of the Middle East and Africa. I would have liked to have met more refugees, but this has not been possible. You represent hundreds of your peers, many of whom are exiles and refugees who are helped every day by the Salesians. I wish to assure you that I share your sufferings. I hope that my visit, by the grace of God, may offer you some consolation in your difficult situation. Your situation is the sad consequence of brutal conflicts and war, which are always evils and which never solve problems. Rather, they only create new ones.

Refugees, such as yourselves, often find themselves deprived, sometimes for long periods, of basic needs such as a dignified home, health care, education, and work. They have had to abandon not only their material possessions, but above all their freedom, their closeness to family, their homelands and cultural traditions. The degrading conditions in

which so many refugees are forced to live are intolerable! For
this reason, we must do everything possible to eradicate the
causes of this situation. I appeal for greater international cooperation to resolve the conflicts that are causing bloodshed
in your homelands, to counter the other causes which are
driving people to leave their home countries, and to improve
conditions so that people may remain or return home. I encourage all who are working generously and steadfastly for
justice and peace not to lose heart. I ask political leaders to always remember that the great majority of their people long
for peace, even if at times they lack the strength and voice to
demand it.

Dear young people, do not be discouraged. It is easy to
say this, but please make an effort not to be discouraged.
With the help of God, continue to hope in a better future despite the difficulties and obstacles that you are currently facing. The Catholic Church is with you, and one of the ways it
is with you is through the invaluable work of the Salesians.
The Church, in addition to other forms of help, also offers
you the opportunity to see to your education and formation.
Remember always that God does not forget any of his children, and that those who are the smallest and who suffer the
most are closest to the Father's heart.

For my part, together with the whole Church, I will continue to pray to the Lord, asking him to inspire those in lead-
ership so that they will not hesitate to promote justice,
security, and peace and do so in ways that are clear and effective. Through her social and charitable organizations, the
Church will remain at your side and will continue to hold up
your cause before the world.

A United Response

From an Address to the European Parliament
Strasbourg, France, November 25, 2014

There needs to be a united response to the question of migration. We cannot allow the Mediterranean to become a vast cemetery! The boats landing daily on the shores of Europe are filled with men and women who need acceptance and assistance. The absence of mutual support within the European Union runs the risk of encouraging particularistic solutions to the problem, solutions that fail to take into account the human dignity of immigrants, and thus contribute to slave labor and continuing social tensions. Europe will be able to confront the problems associated with immigration only if it is capable of clearly asserting its own cultural identity and enacting adequate legislation to protect the rights of European citizens and ensure the acceptance of immigrants; only if it is capable of adopting fair, courageous, and realistic policies that can assist the countries of origin in their own social and political development and in their efforts to resolve internal conflicts—the principal cause of this phenomenon—rather than adopting policies motivated by self-interest, which increase and feed such conflicts. We need to take action against the causes and not only the effects.

With Jesus at the Center

Address to the Federation of Christian Organizations
for International Volunteer Service
December 4, 2014

Dear brothers and sisters, good morning!

I am pleased to meet with you on the occasion of International Volunteer Day... Your federation, which gathers Christian-based volunteer organizations, performs precious action in the world. It is the image of a Church that rolls up her sleeves and serves brothers and sisters who are in difficulty ... Starting with your Christian identity, you present yourselves as "volunteers in the world," with numerous development initiatives that offer a practical response to the scandals of hunger and war...

Many of the countries where you work know the scandal of war. Working for the development of peoples, you are also cooperating to build peace, seeking with tenacious determination to disarm minds, to draw people near, to build bridges between cultures and religions. Faith will help you to do so, even in the most difficult countries where the spiral of violence seems to leave no room for reason. Your activity in refugee camps is a sign of peace and hope.

There you encounter desperate people, faces marked by oppression, children who hunger for food, for liberty, and for a future. How many people in the world are fleeing from the horrors of war! How many people are being persecuted because of their faith, forced to abandon their homes, their places of worship, their lands, their loved ones! How many lives are being torn apart! How much there is of suffering and of destruction! In light of all this, disciples of Christ do not draw back, do not turn their face away, but seek to take on this painful humanity with closeness and evangelical welcome.

I am thinking of migrants and refugees who seek to leave behind harsh living conditions and every type of danger. Cooperation is needed from everyone, from institutions, NGOs, and ecclesial communities, to promote paths of harmonious coexistence among various people and cultures. It is necessary to provide appropriate reception procedures that do not leave migrants adrift at sea or in the hands of unscrupulous traffickers. At the same time, effective collaboration is necessary among states in order to efficiently regulate and manage migratory movements.

Dear brothers and sisters... I encourage you to persevere with joy on this path of faithfulness to humanity and to God, placing the person of Jesus ever more at the center. He will really help you find the time every day for personal encounter with God in prayer: this will be your strength in the most difficult times of disillusion, loneliness, and misunderstanding.

A Throwaway Culture

Address to Members of the Diplomatic Corps
Accredited to the Holy See
January 12, 2015

Today I wish to repeat a word quite dear to us: peace! It comes to us from the angelic hosts who proclaimed it on Christmas night (cf. Lk 2:14) as a precious gift of God, while at the same time it is a personal and social responsibility that calls for our commitment and concern. But together with peace, the image of the Christmas crèche speaks to us another tragic reality: that of rejection. In some iconographic representations, both in the West and in the East—I think for example of the splendid nativity icon of Andrei Rublev—the Child Jesus is shown lying not in a manger but in a tomb. The image, which is meant to connect the two principal Christian feasts of Christmas and Easter, shows that the joyful acceptance of this new birth is inseparable from the entire drama of Jesus' life, his humiliation and rejection even to death on the cross.

The Christmas stories themselves show us the hardened heart of a humanity that finds it difficult to accept the Child. From the very start, he is cast aside, left out in the cold, forced to be born in a stable since there was no room in the inn (cf. Lk 2:7). If this is how the Son of God was treated, how much more so is it the case with so many of our brothers and sisters! Rejection is an attitude we all share; it makes us see our neighbor not as a brother or sister to be accepted but as unworthy of our attention, a rival, or someone to be bent to our will. This is the mindset that fosters a "throwaway culture" that spares nothing and no one—nature, human beings, even God himself. It gives rise to a humanity filled with pain and constantly torn by tensions and conflicts of every sort.

The personal dimension of rejection is inevitably accompanied by a social dimension, a culture of rejection that severs the deepest and most authentic human bonds, leading to the breakdown of society and spawning violence and death. We see painful evidence of this in the events reported daily in the news...

Together with lives thrown away because of war and disease, there are those of numerous refugees and displaced persons. Once again, the reality can be appreciated by reflecting on the childhood of Jesus, which sheds light on another form of the throwaway culture that harms relationships and causes the breakdown of society. Indeed, because of Herod's brutality, the Holy Family was forced to flee to Egypt, and was able to return only several years later (cf. Mt 2:13–15).

One consequence of the situations of conflict in our world is the flight of thousands of persons from their homeland. At times they leave not so much in search of a better future, but in search any future at all, since remaining at home can mean certain death. How many persons lose their lives during these cruel journeys, the victims of unscrupulous and greedy thugs? I raised this issue during my recent visit to the European Parliament, where I insisted that "we cannot allow the Mediterranean to become a vast cemetery" (Address to the European Parliament, Strasbourg, November 25, 2014). Then too there is the alarming fact that many immigrants, especially in the Americas, are unaccompanied children, all the more at risk and in need of even greater care, attention, and protection.

Often coming without documents to strange lands whose language they do not speak, migrants find it difficult to be accepted and to find work. In addition to the uncertainties of their flight, they have to face the drama of rejection. A change of attitude is needed on our part, moving from indifference and fear to genuine acceptance of others. This of course calls for "enacting adequate legislation to protect the rights of . . . citizens and to ensure the acceptance of immigrants" (ibid.). I thank all those who, even at the cost of their lives, are working to assist refugees and immigrants, and I urge states and international organizations to make every effort to resolve these grave humanitarian problems and to provide the immigrants' countries of origin with forms of aid that can help promote their social and political development and settle their internal conflicts, which are the chief cause of this phenomenon. "We need to take action against the causes and not only the effects" (ibid.). This will also enable immigrants to return at some point to their own countries and to contribute to their growth and development.

Prayers for Migrants

A boat full of migrants capsized last night about sixty miles off the Libyan coast and hundreds are feared dead. I express my deepest sorrow in the face of this tragedy and I assure my thoughts and prayers to those still missing and to their families. I address an urgent appeal that the international community will act decisively and promptly to avoid any similar tragedy from happening again. These are men and women like us, our brothers and sisters seeking a better life, starving, persecuted, wounded, exploited, victims of war; they are seeking a better life. They were seeking happiness... I invite you to pray in silence, first, and then all together for these brothers and sisters.

—Regina Coeli, April 19, 2015

Faced with the tragedy of tens of thousands of refugees who flee death from war and hunger, and who have begun a journey moved by hope for survival, the Gospel calls us to be "neighbors" of the smallest and the abandoned, and to give them concrete hope. It's not enough to say, "Take heart. Be patient"... Christian hope has a fighting spirit, with the tenacity of one who goes toward a sure goal.

Therefore, as the Jubilee of Mercy approaches, I make an appeal to parishes, religious communities, monasteries, and shrines throughout Europe, that they express the Gospel in a practical way and host a refugee family. This would be a concrete way of preparing for the Holy Year of Mercy. May every parish, every religious community, every monastery, every shrine of Europe welcome one family, beginning with my diocese of Rome.

I address my brother bishops of Europe, true pastors, that in their dioceses they endorse my appeal, remembering that Mercy is the second name of Love: *"What you have done for the least of my brothers and sisters, that you have done for me"* (cf. Mt 25:46).

In the coming days, the two parishes of the Vatican will also welcome two families of refugees.

—Angelus, September 6, 2015

Immaculate Mother,
For the fifth time I come before you as Bishop of Rome,
to honor you on behalf of all the residents of this city.
We wish to thank you for the constant care
with which you accompany our journey,
the journey of families, of parishes, of religious
    communities;
the journey of those who each day, at times with difficulty,
pass through Rome to go to work;
of the sick, of the elderly, of all the poor,
of so many people who have immigrated here from lands of
    war and hunger.
Thank you because, as soon as we address a thought to you
or a gaze, or a quick "Hail Mary,"

we always feel your maternal, tender and steadfast
   presence.

O Mother, help this city to develop "antibodies" against
   some of the viruses of our time:
indifference, which says: "It doesn't concern me";
the civic discourtesy that disregards the common good;
fear of those who are different or foreign;
transgression disguised as conformity;
the hypocrisy of accusing others while we do the same
   things;
resignation to environmental and ethical decay;
the exploitation of countless men and women.
Help us to reject these and other viruses with the antibodies
   that come from the Gospel.
Help us to develop the good habit of reading a passage
   from the Gospel each day
and, following your example, to cherish the Word in our
   hearts,
so that, as a good seed, it may bear fruit in our lives...

Thank you, O Mother, for always listening to us!
May you bless the Church that is in Rome,
bless this city and the entire world.
Amen.

—*Solemnity of the Immaculate Conception of the Blessed Virgin Mary*
Rome, Spanish Steps, December 8, 2017

A Land of Dreams

Remarks from the Pope's Visit to the United States
September 2015

With [regard to] immigrants: I ask you to excuse me if in some way I am pleading my own case. The church in the United States knows like few others the hopes present in the hearts of these "pilgrims." From the beginning you have learned their languages, promoted their cause, made their contributions your own, defended their rights, helped them to prosper, and kept alive the flame of their faith. Even today, no American institution does more for immigrants than your Christian communities.

Now you are facing this stream of Latin immigration that affects many of your dioceses. Not only as the bishop of Rome, but also as a pastor from the South, I feel the need to thank and encourage you. Perhaps it will not be easy for you to look into their souls; perhaps you will be challenged by their diversity. But know that they also possess resources meant to be shared. So do not be afraid to welcome them. Offer them the warmth of the love of Christ and you will unlock the mystery of their heart. I am certain that, as so often in the past, these people will enrich America and its church.

—*From a Speech to Bishops of the United States, Washington DC, September 23, 2015*

I think of the march that Martin Luther King led from Selma to Montgomery fifty years ago as part of the campaign to fulfill his "dream" of full civil and political rights for African Americans. That dream continues to inspire us all. I am happy that America continues to be, for many, a land of "dreams." Dreams that lead to action, to participation, to commitment. Dreams that awaken what is deepest and truest in the life of a people.

In recent centuries, millions of people came to this land to pursue their dream of building a future in freedom. We, the people of this continent, are not fearful of foreigners, because most of us were once foreigners. I say this to you as the son of immigrants, knowing that so many of you are also descended from immigrants. Tragically, the rights of those who were here long before us were not always respected. For those peoples and their nations, from the heart of American democracy, I wish to reaffirm my highest esteem and appreciation. The first contacts were often turbulent and violent, but it is difficult to judge the past by the criteria of the present. Nonetheless, when the stranger in our midst appeals to us, we must not repeat the sins and the errors of the past. We must resolve now to live as nobly and as justly as possible, as we educate new generations not to turn their back on our "neighbors" and everything around us. Building a nation calls us to recognize that we must constantly relate to others, rejecting a mindset of hostility in order to adopt one of reciprocal subsidiarity, in a constant effort to do our best. I am confident that we can do this.

Our world is facing a refugee crisis of a magnitude not seen since the Second World War. This presents us with great challenges and many hard decisions. On this continent, too, thousands of persons are led to travel north in search of a better life for themselves and for their loved ones, in search of greater opportunities. Is this not what we want for our own children? We must not be taken aback by their numbers, but rather view them as persons, seeing their faces and listening to their stories, trying to respond as best we can to their situation. To respond in a way that is always humane, just, and fraternal. We need to avoid a common temptation nowadays: to discard whatever proves troublesome. Let us remember the Golden Rule: "Do unto others as you would have them do unto you" (Mt 7:12).

This rule points us in a clear direction. Let us treat others with the same passion and compassion with which we want to be treated. Let us seek for others the same possibilities that we seek for ourselves. Let us help others to grow, as we would like to be helped ourselves. In a word, if we want security, let us give security; if we want life, let us give life; if we want opportunities, let us provide opportunities. The yardstick we use for others will be the yardstick that time will use for us.

—*From an Address to a Joint Session of the U.S. Congress*
United States Capitol, Washington, DC, September 24, 2015

A Tragic Exodus

Address to Members of the Jesuit Refugee Service
November 14, 2015

Dear brothers and sisters,

I am happy to receive you on this, the thirty-fifth anniversary of the establishment of the Jesuit Refugee Service envisaged by Fr. Pedro Arrupe, then the superior general of the Society of Jesus. The profound impact made on him by the plight of the South-Vietnamese boat people, exposed to pirate attacks and storms in the South China Sea, was what led him to undertake this initiative.

Fr. Arrupe, who had lived through the atomic bombing of Hiroshima, realized the scope of that tragic exodus of refugees. He saw it as a challenge that the Jesuits could not ignore if they were to remain faithful to their vocation. He wanted the Jesuit Refugee Service to meet both the human and the spiritual needs of refugees, not only their immediate need for food and shelter but also their need to see their human dignity respected, to be listened to and comforted.

The phenomenon of forced migration has dramatically increased since then. Crowds of refugees are leaving different countries of the Middle East, Africa, and Asia to seek refuge in Europe. The United Nations High Commissioner for Refugees has estimated that there are, worldwide, almost sixty million refugees, the highest number since the Second World War. Behind these statistics are people, each of them with a name, a face, a story, an inalienable dignity that belongs to each of them as a child of God.

At present, you are active in ten different regions, with projects in 45 countries, through which you provide services to refugees and peoples in internal migrations. A group of Jesuits and women religious work alongside many lay associates and a great number of refugees. In all this time, you have remained faithful to the ideal of Fr. Arrupe and to the three basic goals of your mission: to accompany, to serve, and to defend the rights of refugees.

The decision to be present in areas of greatest need, in conflict and post-conflict zones, has brought you international recognition for your closeness to people and your ability to learn from this how better to serve. I think especially of your groups in Syria, Afghanistan, the Central African Republic, and the eastern part of the Democratic Republic of Congo, where you accept men and women of different religious beliefs who share your mission.

The Jesuit Refugee Service works to offer hope and prospects to refugees, mainly through the educational services you provide, which reach large numbers of people and are of particular importance. Offering an education is about much more than dispensing concepts. It is something that provides refugees with the wherewithal to progress beyond survival, to keep alive the flame of hope, to believe in the future and to make plans. To give a child a seat at school is the finest gift you can give. All your projects have this ultimate aim: to help refugees to grow in self-confidence, to realize their highest inherent potential and to be able to defend their rights as individuals and communities.

For children forced to emigrate, schools are places of freedom. In the classroom, they are cared for and protected by their teachers. Sadly, we know that even schools are not spared from attacks instigated by those who sow violence. Yet they are places of sharing together with children of other cultural, ethnic, and religious backgrounds; places that follow a set pace and provide a reassuring discipline, places in which children can once more feel "normal" and where parents can be happy to send them.

Education affords young refugees a way to discover their true calling and to develop their potential. Yet all too many refugee children and young people do not receive a quality education. Access to education is limited, especially for girls and in the case of secondary schools. For this reason, during the approaching Jubilee Year of Mercy, you have set the goal of helping another hundred thousand young refugees receive schooling. Your initiative of "Global Education," with its motto "Mercy in Motion," will help you reach many other students who urgently need an education that can help keep them safe. I am grateful to the group of supporters and benefactors and the international development group of the Jesuit Refugee Service who are with us today. Thanks to their energy and support, the Lord's mercy will reach an even larger number of children and their families in the future.

As you persevere in this work of providing education for refugees, think of the Holy Family, Our Lady, St. Joseph, and the Child Jesus, who fled to Egypt to escape violence and to find refuge among strangers. Remember too the words of Jesus: "Blessed are the merciful, for they shall obtain mercy" (Mt 5:7). Take these words with you always, so that they can bring you encouragement and consolation. As for me, I assure you of my prayers. I ask you also, please, do not forget to pray for me.

Humanity on the Move

Address to Members of the Diplomatic Corps
Accredited to the Holy See
January 11, 2016

Dear Ambassadors,

An individualistic spirit is fertile soil for the growth of that kind of indifference toward our neighbors that leads to viewing them in purely economic terms, to a lack of concern for their humanity, and ultimately to feelings of fear and cynicism. Are these not the attitudes we often adopt toward the poor, the marginalized, and the "least" of society? And how many of these "least" do we have in our societies! Among them I think primarily of migrants, with their burden of hardship and suffering, as they seek daily—often in desperation—a place to live in peace and dignity.

Today, then, I would like to reflect with you on the grave crisis of migration that we are facing, in order to discern its causes, to consider possible solutions, and to overcome the inevitable fears associated with this massive and formidable phenomenon, which in 2015 has mainly concerned Europe, but has also affected various regions of Asia and North and Central America.

"Be not frightened, neither be dismayed; for the Lord your God is with you wherever you go" (Josh 1:9). This is the promise that God makes to Joshua, revealing his concern for every person, but particularly for those in precarious situations, such as people seeking refuge in a foreign country. The Bible as a whole recounts the history of a humanity on the move, for mobility is part of our human nature. Human history is made up of countless migrations, sometimes resulting from an awareness of the right to choose freely, and often dictated by external circumstances. From the banishment from Eden to Abraham's journey to the promised land, from the Exodus story to the deportation to Babylon, sacred scripture describes the struggles and sufferings, the desires and hopes that are shared by the hundreds of thousands of persons on the move today, possessed of the same determination that Moses had to reach a land flowing with "milk and honey" (cf. Ex 3:17), a land of freedom and peace.

Now, as then, we hear Rachel weeping for her children who are no more (cf. Jer 31:15; Mt 2:18). Hers is the plea of thousands of people who weep as they flee horrific wars, persecutions, and human rights violations or political or social instability, which often make it impossible for them to live in their native lands. It is the outcry of those forced to flee in order to escape unspeakable acts of cruelty toward vulnerable persons, such as children and the disabled, or martyrdom solely on account of their religion.

Now, as then, we hear Jacob saying to his sons: "Go down and buy grain for us there, that we may live and not die" (Gen 42:2). His is the voice of all those who flee extreme poverty, the inability to feed their families or to receive medical care and education, hopeless squalor or the effects of climate change and extreme weather conditions. Sadly, we know that hunger continues to be one of the gravest plagues of our world, leading to the death of millions of children every year. It is painful to realize that often migrants are not included in international systems of protection based on international agreements.

How can we not see in all this the effects of that "culture of waste" which endangers the human person, sacrificing men and women before the idols of profit and consumption? It is a grievous fact that we grow so inured to situations of poverty and need, to the tragedies affecting so many lives, that they appear "normal." Persons are no longer seen as having preeminent value, to be cared for and respected, especially when poor or disabled, or "not yet useful"—like the unborn—or "no longer needed"—like the elderly. We have grown indifferent to all sorts of waste, starting with the waste of food, which is all the more deplorable when so many individuals and families suffer hunger and malnutrition.

What is needed is a collective commitment that can decisively turn around the culture of waste and lack of respect for human life, so that no one will feel neglected or forgotten and no further lives will be sacrificed due to lack of resources and, above all, of political will.

Sadly, now as then, we hear the voice of Judah who counsels selling his own brother (cf. Gen 37:26–27). His is the arrogance of the powerful who exploit the weak, reducing them to means for their own personal ends or for strategic and political schemes. Where regular migration is impossible, migrants are often forced to turn to human traffickers or smugglers, even though they are aware that in the course of their journey they may well lose their possessions, their dignity, and even their lives. In this context I once more appeal for an end to trafficking in persons, which turns human beings, especially the weakest and most defenseless, into commodities. The image of all the children who died at sea, victims of human callousness and harsh weather, will remain forever imprinted on our minds and hearts. Those who survive and reach a country that accepts them bear the deep and indelible scars of these experiences, in addition to those left by the atrocities that always accompany wars and violence.

Now, as then, we hear the angel say: "Rise, take the child and his mother, and flee to Egypt, and remain there till I tell you" (Mt 2:13). His is the voice heard by many migrants who would never have left their homeland had they not been forced to. Among these are many Christians who in great numbers have abandoned their native lands these past years, despite the fact that they have dwelt there from the earliest days of Christianity.

Finally, we also hear today the voice of the Psalmist: "By the waters of Babylon, there we sat down and wept, when we remembered Zion" (Ps 137:1). His is the cry of those who would readily return to their own country, if only they could find there adequate conditions of security and sustenance. Here too my thoughts turn to the Christians of the Middle East, who desire to contribute fully as citizens to the spiritual and material well-being of their respective nations.

Many of the causes of migration could have been addressed some time ago. So many disasters could have been prevented, or at least their harshest effects mitigated. Today too, before it is too late, much could be done to end such tragedies and to build peace. But that would mean rethinking entrenched habits and practices, beginning with issues involving the arms trade, the provision of raw materials and energy, investment, policies of financing and sustainable development, and even the grave scourge of corruption. We all know, too, that with regard to migration there is a need for mid-term and long-term planning that is not limited to emergency responses. Such planning should include effective assistance for integrating migrants in their receiving countries while also promoting the development of their countries of origin through policies inspired by solidarity, yet not linking assistance to ideological strategies and practices alien or contrary to the cultures of the peoples being assisted.

Without overlooking other dramatic situations—in this regard, I think particularly of the border between Mexico and the United States of America, which I will be near when I visit Ciudad Juárez next month—my thoughts turn in a special way to Europe. Over the past year Europe has witnessed a great wave of refugees—many of whom died in the attempt to migrate—a wave unprecedented in recent history, not even after the end of the Second World War. Many migrants from Asia and Africa see in Europe a beacon for principles such as equality before the law and for values inherent in human nature, including the inviolable dignity and equality of every person, love of neighbor regardless of origin or affiliation, freedom of conscience, and solidarity toward our fellow men and women.

All the same, the massive number of arrivals on the shores of Europe appear to be overburdening the system of reception painstakingly built on the ashes of the Second World War, a system that is still an acknowledged beacon of humanity. Given the immense influx and the inevitable problems it creates, a number of questions have been raised about the real possibilities for accepting and accommodating people, about changes in the cultural and social structures of the receiving countries, and about the reshaping of certain regional geopolitical balances. Equally significant are fears about security, further exacerbated by the growing threat of international terrorism. The present wave of migration seems to be undermining the foundations of that "humanistic spirit" which Europe has always valued and defended. Yet there should be no loss of the values and principles of humanity, respect for the dignity of every person, mutual subsidiarity and solidarity, however much they may prove—in some moments of history—a burden difficult to bear. I wish, then, to reaffirm my conviction that Europe, aided by its great cultural and religious heritage, has the means to defend the centrality of the human person and to find the right balance between its twofold moral responsibility to protect the rights of its citizens and to ensure assistance and acceptance to migrants.

It is important that nations in the forefront of meeting the present emergency not be left to deal alone with the problem, and it is also essential to initiate a frank and respectful dialogue among all the countries involved—countries of origin, transit, and reception—so that, with greater boldness and creativity, new and sustainable solutions can be sought. As things presently stand, there is no place for autonomous solutions pursued by individual states, since the consequences of the decisions made by each inevitably have repercussions on the entire international community. Indeed, migrations, more than ever before, will play a pivotal role in the future of our world, and our response can only be the fruit of a common effort respectful of human dignity and the rights of persons. The Development Agenda adopted last September by the United Nations for the next fifteen years, which deals with many of the problems causing migration, and other documents of the international community on handling the issue of migration, will be able to find application consistent with expectations if they are able to put the person at the center of political decisions at every level, seeing humanity as one family, and all people as brothers and sisters, with respect for mutual differences and convictions of conscience.

In facing the issue of migration, one cannot overlook its cultural implications, beginning with those linked to religious affiliation. Extremism and fundamentalism find fertile soil not only in the exploitation of religion for purposes of power, but also in the vacuum of ideals and the loss of identity—including religious identity—that dramatically marks the so-called West. This vacuum gives rise to the fear which leads to seeing the other as a threat and an enemy, to closed-mindedness and intransigence in defending preconceived notions. The phenomenon of migration raises a serious cultural issue that necessarily demands a response. The acceptance of migrants can thus prove a good opportunity for new understanding and broader horizons, both on the part of those accepted, who have the responsibility to respect the values, traditions, and laws of the community that takes them in, and on the part of the latter, who are called to acknowledge the beneficial contribution each immigrant can make to the whole community. In this context, the Holy See reaffirms its commitment in the ecumenical and interreligious sectors to inaugurating a sincere and respectful dialogue which, by valuing the distinctness and identity of each individual, can foster a harmonious coexistence among all the members of society.

Crossing Borders

Homily in Ciudad Juárez, Mexico
February 17, 2016

In the second century St. Irenaeus wrote that the glory of God is the life of man. It is an expression that continues to echo in the heart of the Church. The glory of the Father is the life of his sons and daughters. There is no greater glory for a father than to see his children blossom, no greater satisfaction than to see his children grow up, develop, and flourish.

This word echoes forcefully today among us; this word is the voice crying out in the wilderness, inviting us to conversion. In this Year of Mercy, with you here, I beg for God's mercy; with you I wish to plead for the gift of tears, the gift of conversion...

Here in Ciudad Juárez, as in other border areas, there are thousands of immigrants from Central America and other countries, not to speak of the many Mexicans who also seek to pass over "to the other side." Each step of the journey laden with grave injustices: the enslaved, the imprisoned and extorted; so many of these brothers and sisters of ours suffer the consequences of a trade in human trafficking, the trafficking of persons.

We cannot deny the humanitarian crisis that in recent years has meant migration for thousands of people, whether by train or highway or on foot, crossing hundreds of kilometers through mountains, deserts, and inhospitable zones. The human tragedy that is forced migration is a global phenomenon today. This crisis, which can be measured in numbers and statistics, we want instead to measure with names, stories, families. These brothers and sisters of our have been expelled by poverty· and violence, by drug trafficking and criminal organizations. Faced with so many legal vacuums, they get caught up in a web that ensnares and always destroys the poorest. Not only do they suffer poverty but they must also endure all these forms of violence. Injustice is radicalized in the young; they are "cannon fodder," persecuted and threatened when they try to flee the spiral of violence and the hell of drugs. And what can we say about the many women whose lives have been violently expropriated?

Let us together ask our God for the gift of conversion, the gift of tears, let us ask him to give us open hearts like those of the Ninevites, open to his call in the suffering faces of countless men and women. No more death! No more exploitation! There is always time to change, always a way out and always an opportunity, there is always the time to implore the mercy of God.

Just as in Jonas's time, so too today may we commit ourselves to conversion; may we be signs lighting the way and announcing salvation. I know of the work of countless civil organizations working to support the rights of migrants. I know too of the committed work of so many men and women religious, priests, and lay people in accompanying migrants and in defending life. They are on the front lines, often risking their own lives. By their very lives they are prophets of mercy; they are the beating heart and the accompanying feet of the Church that opens her arms and sustains.

This time for conversion, this time for salvation, is the time for mercy. And so, let us say together in response to the suffering on so many: In your compassion and mercy, Lord, have pity on us... cleanse us from our sins and create in us a pure heart, a new spirit (cf. Ps 51[50]:3, 4, 12).

And now I also want to greet from here all our beloved brothers and sisters who are joining us simultaneously on the other side of the border, especially those who are gathered in the Stadium of the University of El Paso, known as the Sun Bowl, under the guidance of your bishop, Mark Seitz. Thanks to technology, we can pray, sing, and celebrate together the merciful love that God gives us, and that no border can prevent us from sharing. Thank you, brothers and sisters of El Paso, for making us feel one single family and one same Christian community.

Do Not Lose Hope!

Mòria Refugee Camp, Lesbos, Greece
April 16, 2016

Dear Brothers and Sisters,

I have wanted to be with you today. I want to tell you that you are not alone. In these weeks and months, you have endured much suffering in your search for a better life. Many of you felt forced to flee situations of conflict and persecution for the sake, above all, of your children, your little ones. You have made great sacrifices for your families. You know the pain of having left behind everything that is dear to you and—what is perhaps most difficult—not knowing what the future will bring. Many others like you are also in camps or towns, waiting, hoping to build a new life on this continent.

I have come here with my brothers, Patriarch Bartholomew and Archbishop Ieronymos, simply to be with you and to hear your stories. We have come to call the attention of the world to this grave humanitarian crisis and to plead for its resolution. As people of faith, we wish to join our voices to speak out on your behalf. We hope that the world will heed these scenes of tragic and indeed desperate need, and respond in a way worthy of our common humanity.

God created humanity to be one family; when any of our brothers and sisters suffer, we are all affected. We all know from experience how easy it is for some to ignore other people's suffering and even to exploit their vulnerability. But we also know that these crises can bring out the very best in us. You have seen this among yourselves and among the Greek people, who have generously responded to your needs amid their own difficulties. You have also seen it in the many people, especially the young from throughout Europe and the world, who have come to help you. Yes, so much more needs to be done! But let us thank God that in our suffering he never leaves us alone. There is always someone who can reach out and help us.

This is the message I want to leave with you today: Do not lose hope! The greatest gift we can offer one another is love: a merciful look, a readiness to listen and understand, a word of encouragement, a prayer. May you share this gift with one another. We Christians love to tell the story of the Good Samaritan, a foreigner who saw a man in need and immediately stopped to help. For us, it is a story about God's mercy, which is meant for everyone, for God is the All-Merciful. It is also a summons to show that same mercy to those in need. May all our brothers and sisters on this continent, like the Good Samaritan, come to your aid in the spirit of fraternity, solidarity, and respect for human dignity that has distinguished its long history.

Dear brothers and sisters, may God bless all of you and, in a special way, your children, the elderly, and all those who suffer in body and spirit! I embrace all of you with affection. Upon you and upon those who accompany you, I invoke his gifts of strength and peace.

Solidarity and Mercy

Address to Members of the European Confederation
and of the World Union of Jesuit Alumni and Alumnae
September 17, 2016

Tragically, at present, more than sixty-five million persons are forcibly displaced around the globe. This unprecedented number is beyond all imagination. The displaced population of today's world is now larger than the entire population of Italy! If we move beyond mere statistics, however, we will discover that refugees are women and men, boys and girls who are no different from our own family members and friends. Each of them has a name, a face, and a story, as well as an inalienable right to live in peace and to aspire to a better future for their sons and daughters...

More than ever today, as war rages all across God's creation, as record numbers of refugees die trying to cross the Mediterranean Sea—which has become a cemetery—and as refugees spend years and years languishing in camps, the Church needs you to draw on the bravery and example of Father Pedro Arrupe. Through your Jesuit education, you have been invited to become "companions of Jesus" and, with Saint Ignatius Loyola as your guide, you have been sent into the world to be women and men for and with others. At this place and time in history, there is great need for men and women who hear the cry of the poor and respond with mercy and generosity.

At the close of World Youth Day in Krakow a few weeks ago, I told the youth gathered there to be brave. As graduates of Jesuit schools, you also must know how to be brave in responding to the needs of refugees in today's world. It will help you to recall your Ignatian roots as you address the problems experienced by refugees. You must offer the Lord "all your liberty, your memory, your understanding and your entire will" as you continue to understand the causes of forced migration and serve refugees in your countries.

Throughout this Year of Mercy, the Holy Door of Saint Peter's Basilica has remained open as a reminder that God's mercy is offered to all those in need, now and always. Millions of the faithful have made the pilgrimage to the Holy Door here and in churches throughout the world, recalling that God's mercy lasts forever and reaches out to all. Also, with your help, the Church will be able to respond more fully to the human tragedy of refugees through acts of mercy that promote their integration into the European context and beyond. And so I encourage you to welcome refugees into your homes and communities, so that their first encounter with Europe is not the traumatic experience of sleeping cold on the streets, but rather one of warm human welcome. Remember that authentic hospitality is a profound gospel value that nurtures love and is our greatest security against hateful acts of terrorism.

Sometimes we can feel that we are alone as we try to put mercy into action. Know, however, that you join your work with that of many ecclesial organizations that work for humanitarian causes and that dedicate themselves to the excluded and marginalized. Even more important, remember that the love of God accompanies you in this work. You are God's eyes, mouth, hands, and heart in this world.

I thank you for stepping into the difficult issues involved in welcoming refugees. While refugees find many doors closed to them, many doors have been opened for you through your Jesuit education. You have learned much from the refugees you have met. As you leave Rome and return home, I urge you to help transform your communities into places of welcome where all God's children have the opportunity not simply to survive, but to grow, flourish, and bear fruit.

And as you persevere in this faithful work of providing welcome and education for refugees, think of the Holy Family—Mary, Joseph, and the Child Jesus—on their long journey to Egypt as refugees, fleeing violence and finding refuge among strangers. Remember as well the words of Jesus: "For I was hungry and you gave me food, I was thirsty and you gave me drink, a stranger and you welcomed me" (Mt 25:35). Take these words and these gestures with you today. May they bring you encouragement and consolation. As for me, assuring you of my prayers, I ask you also, please, do not forget to pray for me. Thank you!

"A Stranger and
You Welcomed Me"

*General Audience, St. Peter's Square
October 26, 2016*

Dear Brothers and Sisters,

Let us continue to reflect on the corporal works of mercy, which the Lord Jesus gave us in order to keep our faith ever alive and dynamic. These works, indeed, show that Christians are not weary and idle as they await the final encounter with the Lord but each day go to meet him, recognizing his face in those of the many people who ask for help. Today let us concentrate on these words of Jesus: "I was a stranger and you welcomed me, I was naked and you clothed me" (Mt 25:35–36). In our time, charitable action regarding foreigners is more relevant than ever. The economic crisis, armed conflicts, and climate change have forced many people to emigrate. However, migration is not a new phenomenon; it is part of the history of humanity. It is a lack of historical memory to think that this phenomenon has arisen only in recent years.

The Bible offers us many concrete examples of migration. Suffice it to think of Abraham. God's call spurred him to leave his country in order to go to another: "Go from your country and your kindred and your father's house to the land that I will show you" (Gen 12:1). It was so also for the people of Israel, who from Egypt, where they had been slaves, went marching in the desert for forty years until they reached the land promised by God. The Holy Family itself— Mary, Joseph and the baby Jesus—were forced to emigrate in order to escape Herod's threat: Joseph "rose and took the child and his mother by night, and departed to Egypt, and remained there until the death of Herod" (Mt 2:14–15). The history of humanity is a history of migrations: throughout our entire world, there is no people that has not known the migratory phenomenon.

Over the course of the centuries we have witnessed, in this regard, great expressions of solidarity, although there has been no lack of social tension. Today, the context of the economic crisis unfortunately fosters the emergence of attitudes of closure and not of welcome. In some parts of the world walls and barriers are going up. At times it seems that the silent work of so many men and women who, in various ways, do all they can to help and assist the refugees and migrants is obscured by the clamor of others who give voice to an instinctive selfishness. However, closure is not a solution, but instead ends up fostering criminal trafficking. The only path to a solution is through solidarity. Solidarity with the migrant, solidarity with the foreigner...

The commitment of Christians in this field is as urgent today as it was in the past. Looking only at the last century, we recall the splendid figure of Saint Frances Cabrini, who, along with her companions, dedicated her life to immigrants to the United States of America. Today too we need these witnesses so that mercy may reach the many who are in need. It is a commitment that involves everyone, without exception. We all, dioceses, parishes, institutes of consecrated life, associations and movements, and individual Christians, are called to welcome our brothers and sisters who are fleeing from war, from hunger, from violence and from inhuman living conditions. All together we are a great supportive force for those who have lost their homelands, families, work, and dignity.

Several days ago, a little story unfolded in the city. There was a refugee who was looking for a street and a lady approached him and said: "Are you looking for something?" That refugee had no shoes, and he said: "I would like to go to Saint Peter's to enter the Holy Door." And the lady thought: "But he has no shoes, how will he manage to walk there?" So she called a taxi. But the migrant, that refugee, had a disagreeable odor and the taxi driver at first didn't want him to get in the car, but in the end he relented. And the lady, sitting next to the refugee during the ride, asked him a little about his history as a migrant: it took ten minutes to get here to St. Peter's. This man told his story of suffering, of war, of hunger because he had fled from his homeland in order to migrate. When they arrived at their destination, the lady opened her purse to pay the taxi driver—who at first had not wanted this immigrant in his cab because he smelled—told her: "No, ma'am, I should be paying you because you made me listen to a story that has changed my heart." This lady understood what a migrant's pain is, because she was of Armenian descent and knew the suffering of her people. When we do something like this, at first we refuse because it causes us a little inconvenience, "But...he smells..." In the end, the episode gives fragrance to our soul and changes us. Let us think about this story and consider what we can do for refugees...

Dear brothers and sisters, let us not fall into the trap of closing in on ourselves, indifferent to the needs of brothers and sisters and concerned only with our own interests. It is precisely in the measure to which we open ourselves to others that life becomes fruitful, society regains peace, and people recover their full dignity. Do not forget that lady, do not forget that migrant who had a disagreeable odor, and do not forget that driver whose spirit was changed by the immigrant.

Migrants Are Persons

Address to Members of the Diplomatic Corps
Accredited to the Holy See
January 9, 2017

Last year the international community gathered at two important events convened by the United Nations: the first World Humanitarian Summit and the Summit for Refugees and Migrants. With regard to migrants, displaced persons and refugees, a common commitment is needed, one focused on offering them a dignified welcome. This would involve respecting the right of "every human being...to emigrate to other countries and take up residence there," while at the same time ensuring that migrants can be integrated into the societies in which they are received without the latter sensing that their security, cultural identity, and political-social stability are threatened. On the other hand, immigrants themselves must not forget that they have a duty to respect the laws, culture, and traditions of the countries that receive them.

Prudence on the part of public authorities does not mean enacting policies of exclusion vis-à-vis migrants, but it does entail evaluating, with wisdom and foresight, the extent to which their country is in a position, without prejudice to the common good of citizens, to offer a decent life to migrants, especially those truly in need of protection. Above all, the current crisis should not be reduced to a simple matter of numbers. Migrants are persons with their own names, stories, and families. There can never be true peace as long as the personal identity of a single human being is violated or any individual is reduced to a mere statistic or an object of economic calculation.

The issue of migration is not one that can leave some countries indifferent while others are left with the burden of humanitarian assistance, often at the cost of notable strain and great hardship in the face of an apparently unending emergency. All should feel responsible for jointly pursuing the international common good through concrete gestures of human solidarity; these are essential building-blocks of that peace and development which entire nations and millions of people still await. So I am grateful to the many countries that offer a generous welcome to those in need, beginning with various European nations, particularly Italy, Germany, Greece, and Sweden.

I vividly remember my visit to the island of Lesbos in the company of my brothers Patriarch Bartholomew and Archbishop Ieronymos. There I saw at first hand the dramatic situation of the refugee camps, but also the goodness and spirit of service shown by the many persons committed to assisting those living there. Nor should we overlook the welcome offered by other countries of Europe and the Middle East, such as Lebanon, Jordan, and Turkey, as well as the commitment of various African and Asian countries. In the course of my visit to Mexico, where I experienced the joy of the Mexican people, I likewise felt close to the thousands of migrants from Central America who, in their attempt to find a better future, endure terrible injustices and dangers as victims of extortion and objects of that deplorable trade—that horrible form of modern slavery—which is human trafficking.

One enemy of peace is a "reductive vision" of the human person, which opens the way to the spread of injustice, social inequality, and corruption. With regard to this last phenomenon, the Holy See has taken on new commitments with its formal adherence, on last September 19, to the United Nations Convention against Corruption, adopted by the General Assembly of the United Nations on October 31, 2003.

In his encyclical *Populorum Progressio*, issued fifty years ago, Blessed Paul VI noted how such situations of inequality provoke conflict. As he stated, "civil progress and economic development are the only road to peace," which public authorities have the duty to encourage and foster by creating conditions for a more equitable distribution of resources and by generating employment opportunities, especially for young people. In today's world, all too many people, especially children, still suffer from endemic poverty and live in conditions of food insecurity—indeed, hunger—even as natural resources are the object of greedy exploitation by a few, and enormous amounts of food are wasted daily.

Children and young people are the future; it is for them that we work and build. They cannot be selfishly overlooked or forgotten. As I stated recently in a letter addressed to all bishops, I consider it a priority to protect children, whose innocence is often violated by exploitation, clandestine, and slave labor, prostitution or the abuse of adults, criminals, and dealers in death.

Justice, Civility, and Solidarity

Address to Participants in the International Forum
on "Migration and Peace"
February 21, 2017

Dear Ladies and Gentlemen,

Migration, in its various forms, is not a new phenomenon in humanity's history. It has left its mark on every age, encouraging encounter between peoples and the birth of new civilizations. In its essence, migration is the expression of that inherent desire for the happiness proper to every human being, a happiness that is to be sought and pursued. For us Christians, all human life is an itinerant journey toward our heavenly homeland.

The beginning of this third millennium is very much characterized by migratory movement which, in terms of origin, transit, and destination, involves nearly every part of the world. Unfortunately, in the majority of cases this movement is forced, caused by conflict, natural disasters, persecution, climate change, violence, extreme poverty, and inhumane living conditions: "The sheer number of people migrating from one continent to another, or shifting places within their own countries and geographical areas, is striking. Contemporary movements of migration represent the largest movement of individuals, if not of peoples, in history" (*Message for the World Day of Migrants and Refugees*, August 5, 2013).

In the face of this complex panorama, I feel the need to express particular concern for the forced nature of many contemporary migratory movements, which increases the challenges presented to the political community, to civil society, and to the Church, and which amplifies the urgency for a coordinated and effective response to these challenges.

Our shared response may be articulated by four verbs: *to welcome, to protect, to promote,* and *to integrate.*

To welcome. "Rejection is an attitude we all share; it makes us see our neighbor not as a brother or sister to be accepted, but as unworthy of our attention, a rival, or someone to be bent to our will" (*Address to the Diplomatic Corps*, January 12, 2015). Faced with this kind of rejection, which is rooted ultimately in self-centeredness and amplified by populist rhetoric, what is needed is a change of attitude to overcome indifference and to counter fears with a generous approach of welcoming those who knock at our doors. For those who flee conflicts and terrible persecutions, often trapped within the grip of criminal organizations that have no scruples, we need to open, accessible, and secure humanitarian channels. A responsible and dignified welcome to our brothers and sisters begins with offering them decent and appropriate shelter. The enormous gathering together of persons seeking asylum and of refugees has not produced positive results. Instead, these gatherings have created new situations of vulnerability and hardship. More widespread programs of welcome, already initiated in different places, seem to favor a personal encounter and allow for greater quality of service and increased guarantees of success.

To protect. My predecessor, Pope Benedict, highlighted the fact that the migratory experience often makes people more vulnerable to exploitation, abuse, and violence (cf. Benedict XVI, *Message for the World Day of Migrants and Refugees*, October 18, 2005). We are speaking about millions of migrant workers, male and female—and among these particularly men and women in irregular situations, those exiled and seeking asylum, and those who are victims of trafficking. Defending their inalienable rights, ensuring their fundamental freedoms, and respecting their dignity are duties from which no one can be exempted. Protecting these brothers and sisters is a moral imperative that translates into adopting juridical instruments, both international and national, that must be clear and relevant; implementing just and far-reaching political choices; prioritizing constructive processes, which perhaps are slower, over immediate results of consensus; implementing timely and humane programs in the fight against "the trafficking of human flesh" that profits from the misfortune of others; coordinating the efforts of all actors, among which, you may be assured will always be the Church.

To promote. Protecting is not enough. What is required is the promotion of the integral human development of migrants, exiles, and refugees. This "takes place by attending to the inestimable goods of justice, peace, and the care of creation" (Apostolic Letter *Humanam Progressionem*, August 17, 2016). Development, according to the social doctrine of the Church (cf. *Compendium of the Social Doctrine of the Church*, 373, 374), is an undeniable right of every human being. As such, it must be guaranteed by ensuring the necessary conditions for its exercise, both in the individual and social context, through the provision of fair access to fundamental goods for all people and offering the possibility of choice and growth. Also here a coordinated effort is needed, one that takes into account all the parties involved: from the political community to civil society, from international organizations to religious institutions. The human promotion of migrants and their families begins with their communities of origin. That is where such promotion should be guaranteed, joined to the right of *being able* to emigrate, as well as the right to *not be constrained* to emigrate (cf. Benedict XVI, *Message for the World Day of Migrants and Refugees*, October 12, 2012), in other words, the right to find in one's own homeland the conditions necessary for living a dignified life. To this end, efforts must be encouraged that lead to the implementation of programs of international cooperation, free from partisan interests, and programs of transnational development that involve migrants as active protagonists.

To integrate. Integration, which is neither assimilation nor incorporation, is a two-way process, rooted essentially in the joint recognition of the other's cultural richness: it is not the superimposition of one culture over another, nor mutual isolation, which carries the insidious and dangerous risk of creating ghettoes. Concerning those who arrive and who are duty bound not to close themselves off from the culture and traditions of the receiving country, respecting above all its laws, the family dimension of the process of integration must not be overlooked. For this reason I feel the need to reiterate the necessity, often presented by the magisterium (cf. John Paul II,

Message for World Migration Day, August 15, 1986), of policies directed at favoring and benefiting the reunion of families. With regard to indigenous populations, they must be supported by helping them to be sufficiently aware of and open to processes of integration which, though not always simple and immediate, are always essential and, for the future, indispensable. This requires specific programs that foster significant encounters with others. Furthermore, for the Christian community, the peaceful integration of persons of various cultures is, in some way, a reflection of its catholicity, since unity, which does not nullify ethnic and cultural diversity, constitutes a part of the life of the Church, which, in the Spirit of Pentecost, is open to all and desires to embrace all (cf. John Paul II, *Message for World Migration Day*, August 5, 1987).

I believe that conjugating these four verbs, in the first person singular and in the first person plural, is today a responsibility, a duty we have toward our brothers and sisters who, for various reasons, have been forced to leave their homeland: a *duty* of *justice*, of *civility*, and of *solidarity*.

First of all, a duty of justice. We can no longer sustain unacceptable economic inequality, which prevents us from applying the principle of the ultimate purpose of the earth's goods. We are all called to undertake processes of apportionment that are respectful, responsible, and inspired by the precepts of distributive justice. "We need, then, to find ways by which all may benefit from the fruits of the earth, not only to avoid the widening gap between those who have more and those who must be content with the crumbs, but above all because it is a question of justice, equality, and respect for every human being" (*Message for the World Day of Peace*, December 8, 2013, 9). One group of individuals cannot control half of the world's resources. We cannot allow for persons and entire peoples to have a right only to gather the remaining crumbs. Nor can we be indifferent or think ourselves dispensed from the moral imperatives that flow from a joint responsibility to care for the planet, a shared responsibility often stressed by the political international community, as also by the magisterium (cf. *Compendium of the Social Doctrine of the Church*, 9, 163, 189, 406). This joint responsibility must be interpreted in accord with the principle of subsidiarity, "which grants freedom to develop the capabilities present at every level of society, while also demanding a greater sense of responsibility for the common good from those who wield greater power" (*Laudato Si'*, 196). Ensuring justice means also reconciling history with our present globalized situation, without perpetuating mindsets that exploit people and places, a consequence of the most cynical use of the market in order to increase the well-being of the few. As Pope Benedict affirmed, the process of decolonization was delayed "both because of new forms of colonialism and continued dependence on old and new foreign powers, and because of grave irresponsibility within the very countries that have achieved independence" (Encyclical Letter *Caritas in Veritate*, 33). For all this there must be redress.

Second, there is a duty of civility. Our commitment to migrants, exiles, and refugees is an application of those principles and values of welcome and fraternity that constitute a common patrimony of humanity and wisdom from which we draw. Such principles and values have been historically codified in the Universal Declaration of Human Rights and in numerous conventions and international agreements. "Every migrant is a human person who, as such, possesses fundamental, inalienable rights that must be respected by everyone and in every circumstance" (62). Today more than ever, it is necessary to affirm the centrality of the human person, without allowing immediate and ancillary circumstances, or even the necessary fulfillment of bureaucratic and administrative requirements, to obscure this essential dignity. As Saint John Paul II stated, an "irregular legal status cannot allow the migrant to lose his dignity, since he is endowed with inalienable rights, which can neither be violated nor ignored" (John Paul II, *Message for World Migration Day*, July 25, 1995, 2). From the duty of civility is also regained the value of fraternity, which is founded on the innate *relational constitution* of the human person: "A lively awareness of our relatedness helps us to look upon and to treat each person as a true sister or brother; without fraternity it is impossible to build a just society and a solid and lasting peace" (*Message for the World Day of Peace*, December 8, 2013, 1). Fraternity is the most civil way of relating with the reality of another person, which does not threaten us but engages, reaffirms, and enriches our individual identity (cf. Benedict XVI, *Address to Participants in an Interacademic Conference on "The Changing Identity of the Individual,"* January 28, 2008).

Finally, there is a duty of solidarity. In the face of tragedies that take the lives of so many migrants and refugees—conflicts, persecutions, abuse, violence, death—expressions of empathy and compassion cannot help but spontaneously well up. "Where is your brother" (Gen 4:9): this question, which God has asked of man from his beginnings, involves us, especially today, with regard to our brothers and sisters who are migrating: "This is not a question directed to others; it is a question directed to me, to you, to each of us" (*Homily at the*

"Arena" Sports Camp, Salina Quarter, Lampedusa, July 8, 2013). Solidarity is born precisely from the capacity to understand the needs of our brothers and sisters who are in difficulty and to take responsibility for these needs. Upon this, in short, is based the sacred value of hospitality found in religious traditions. For us Christians, hospitality offered to the weary traveler is offered to Jesus Christ himself, through the newcomer: "I was a stranger and you welcomed me" (Mt 25:35). The duty of solidarity is to counter throwaway culture and give greater attention to those who are weakest, poorest, and most vulnerable. Thus "a change of attitude toward migrants and refugees is needed on the part of everyone, moving away from attitudes of defensiveness and fear, indifference, and marginalization—all typical of a throwaway culture—toward attitudes based on a culture of encounter, the only culture capable of building a better, more just and fraternal world" (*Message for the World Day of Migrants and Refugees*, August 5, 2013).

As I conclude these reflections, allow me to draw attention again to a particularly vulnerable group of migrants, exiles, and refugees whom we are called to welcome, to protect, to promote, and to integrate. I am speaking of the children and young people who are forced to live far from their homelands and who are separated from their loved ones. I dedicated my most recent message for the World Day of Migrants and Refugees to them, highlighting how "we need to work toward protection, integration, and long-term solutions" (*Message for the World Day of Migrants and Refugees*, September 8, 2016).

I trust that these two days will bear abundant fruit of good works. I assure you of my prayers; and, please, do not forget to pray for me. Thank you.

A Pilgrim People

Address to the National Directors of Pastoral Care for Migrants
of the Catholic Bishops' Conferences of Europe
September 22, 2017

Dear Brothers and Sisters,

I am very grateful to all of you for the great effort you have made in recent years to help the many migrants and refugees who knock at Europe's doors in search of a place of safety and a more dignified life.

The complex and varied phenomenon of continued migration has overwhelmed existing immigration policies and measures for the protection of migrants ratified by international agreements. In the face of this crisis, the Church is committed to remain faithful to her mission "to love Jesus Christ, to adore and love him, particularly in the poorest and most abandoned" (*Message for the World Day of Migrants and Refugees*, 2015).

The Church's maternal love for these, our brothers and sisters, must be concretely shown at every stage of their journey, from start to finish, in such a manner that ecclesial communities and organizations at every step of the way take an active part in this one mission, each to the best of its ability. Seeing and serving the Lord in these members of his "pilgrim people" is a responsibility that unites all dioceses in the effort to provide a constant, coordinated, and effective outreach.

Dear friends, I cannot fail to express my concern about manifestations of intolerance, discrimination, and xenophobia that have appeared in various parts of Europe. Often this reaction is motivated by mistrust and fear of the other, the foreigner, those who are different. I am even more worried about the disturbing fact that our Catholic communities in Europe are not exempt from these defensive and negative reactions, supposedly justified by a vague moral obligation to preserve an established religious and cultural identity.

The Church has spread to all continents thanks to the "migration" of missionaries convinced of the universality of the saving message of Jesus Christ, meant for men and women of every culture. Throughout the history of the Church, there have been temptations to exclusivity and cultural rigidity, but the Holy Spirit has always helped overcome these temptations by ensuring constant openness to others, viewed as a positive opportunity for growth and enrichment.

I am sure that the Holy Spirit also helps us today to maintain a confident attitude of openness, capable of surmounting every barrier and breaking down every wall.

In listening attentively to the dioceses in Europe, I sense a deep unease about the massive influx of migrants and refugees. That unease needs to be acknowledged and appreciated in the light of this moment of history, marked as it is by an economic crisis that has left deep wounds. The situation been aggravated by the sheer size and makeup of the continuing waves of migrants, by the general unpreparedness of the countries that receive them, and by often inadequate national and community policies. But the unease is also indicative of the limits of the process of European unification and points up the obstacles hindering the concrete application of universal human rights and the expression of that integral humanism which is among the finest fruits of European civilization. For Christians, all these factors must be interpreted, in opposition to a self-enclosed and secularist mentality, in the light of the unique, God-given dignity of each human person.

From a distinctively ecclesiological perspective, the arrival of great numbers of our brothers and sisters in the faith offers the churches in Europe yet another opportunity to embody fully that catholicity which, as we profess in the Creed each Sunday, is a fundamental mark of the Church. In recent years, many dioceses in Europe have already found themselves enriched by the presence of Catholic immigrants who have brought with them their devotions and their liturgical and apostolic enthusiasm.

From a missionary perspective, the current influx of migrants can be seen as a new "frontier" for mission, a privileged opportunity to proclaim Jesus Christ and the gospel message at home, and to bear concrete witness to the Christian faith in a spirit of charity and profound esteem for other religious communities. The encounter with migrants and refugees of other denominations and religions represents fertile ground for the growth of open and enriching ecumenical and interreligious dialogue...

May the spirit of communion in reflection and action be a source of strength for all of you, since challenges faced alone always appear more daunting. May your voice continue to be timely and prophetic, and, above all, grounded in actions consistent with, and inspired by, the principles of Christian doctrine.

Once again, I express my appreciation for your generous commitment to the complex and urgent work of offering pastoral care to migrants. I assure you of my prayers for your intentions, and I ask you, please, not to forget to pray for me.

Loving the Other, the Stranger, as Ourselves

Homily for World Day of Migrants and Refugees
Vatican Basilica, January 14, 2018

This year I wanted to celebrate the World Day of Migrants and Refugees with a Mass that invites and welcomes you especially who are migrants, refugees, and asylum seekers. Some of you have recently arrived in Italy, others are long-time residents and work here, and still others make up the so-called "second-generation."

For everyone in this assembly, the Word of God has resonated and today invites us to deepen the special call that the Lord addresses to each one of us. As he did with Samuel (cf. 1 Sam 3:3b–10, 19), he calls us by name—each one of us—and asks us to honor the fact that each of us has been created a unique and unrepeatable being, each different from the others and each with a singular role in the history of the world. In the Gospel (cf. Jn 1:35–42), the two disciples of John ask Jesus, "Where do you live?" (v. 38), implying that the reply to this question would determine their judgment upon the master from Nazareth. The response of Jesus is clear—*"Come and see!"* (v. 39)—and opens the door to a personal encounter which requires sufficient time to *welcome, to know,* and *to acknowledge* the other.

In the message for this year's World Day of Migrants and Refugees I have written, "Every stranger who knocks at our door is an opportunity for an encounter with Jesus Christ, who identifies with the welcomed and rejected strangers of every age (Mt 25:35, 43)." And for the stranger, the migrant, the refugee, the asylum seeker, and the displaced person, every door in a new land is also an opportunity to encounter Jesus. His invitation to "come and see" is addressed today to all of us, to local communities and to new arrivals. It is an invitation to overcome our fears so as to encounter the other, to welcome, to know, and to acknowledge him or her. It is an invitation that offers the opportunity to draw near to the other and see where and how he or she lives. In today's world, for new arrivals to welcome, to know, and to acknowledge means to know and respect the laws, the culture, and the traditions of the countries that take them in. It even includes understanding their fears and apprehensions for the future. And for local communities to welcome, to know, and to acknowledge newcomers means to open themselves without prejudices to the rich diversity of these newcomers, to understand the hopes and potential of the newly arrived as well as their fears and vulnerabilities.

True encounter with the other does not end with welcome, but involves us all in the three further actions that I spelled out in the message for this day: *to protect, to promote,* and *to integrate.* In the true encounter with the neighbor, are we capable of recognizing Jesus Christ who is asking to be welcomed, protected, promoted, and integrated? As the gospel parable of the final judgment teaches us: the Lord was hungry, thirsty, naked, sick, a stranger, and in prison—by some he was helped and by others not (cf. Mt 25:31–46). This true encounter with Christ is the source of salvation, a salvation that should be announced and brought to all, as the apostle Andrew shows us. After revealing to his brother Simon, "We have found the Messiah" (Jn 1:41), Andrew brings him to Jesus so that Simon can have the same experience of encounter.

It is not easy to enter into another culture, to put oneself in the shoes of people so different from us, to understand their thoughts and their experiences. As a result, we often refuse to encounter the other and raise barriers to defend ourselves. Local communities are sometimes afraid that the newly arrived will disturb the established order, will "steal" something they have long labored to build up. And the newly arrived also have fears: they are afraid of confrontation, judgment, discrimination, failure. These fears are legitimate, based on doubts that are fully comprehensible from a human point of view. Having doubts and fears is not a sin. The sin is to allow these fears to determine our responses, to limit our choices, to compromise respect and generosity, to feed hostility and rejection. The sin is to refuse to encounter the other, the different, the neighbor, when this is in fact a privileged opportunity to encounter the Lord.

From this encounter with Jesus present in the poor, the rejected, the refugee, the asylum seeker flows our prayer of today. It is a reciprocal prayer: migrants and refugees pray for local communities, and local communities pray for the newly arrived and for migrants who have been here longer. To the maternal intercession of Mary Most Holy we entrust the hopes of all the world's migrants and refugees and the aspirations of the communities that welcome them. In this way, responding to the supreme commandment of charity and love of neighbor, may we all learn to love the other, the stranger, as ourselves.

A Merciful Gaze

*Meeting with the Sant'Egidio Community
on the Fiftieth Anniversary of Its Foundation
March 11, 2018*

Dear Friends,

Thank you for your welcome! I am pleased to be here with you for the fiftieth anniversary of the Community of Sant'Egidio...You did not wish to make this festivity merely a celebration of the past, but also and above all a joyous manifestation of responsibility in the future. This makes us think of the gospel parable of the talents, which speaks of a man who, "going on a journey, called his servants and entrusted to them his property" (Mt 25:14). To each of you too, whatever your age, is given at least one talent. Upon it is inscribed the charism of this community, a charism which, when I came here in 2014, I summed up in these words: *prayer, the poor, and peace.* The three "Ps." And I added: "As you walk this path, you help compassion grow in the heart of society—which is the true revolution, that of compassion and tenderness, which rises from the heart—to cultivate friendship in place of the ghosts of animosity and indifference."

Prayer, the poor, and peace are the talents of the community, talents that have grown over fifty years. You receive them once again today with joy. In the parable, however, a servant hides his talent in a hole and justifies himself thus: "I was afraid and went and hid your talent in the ground" (v. 25). This man did not know how to invest his talent in the future, because he allowed himself to be guided by fear.

The world today is often overcome by *fear*—also by anger which is the sister of fear… It is an ancient disease: in the Bible the invitation not to be afraid is often repeated. Our age is marked by great fears in the face of the vast scale of globalization. And fears often focus on those who are foreigners, different from us, poor, as if they were an enemy. Nations' development plans are also driven by opposition to these people. And thus we defend ourselves from them, believing we are preserving what we have or who we are. The atmosphere of fear can also infect Christians who, like that servant in the parable, hide the gift they have received: they do not invest it in the future; they do not share it with others, but they keep it for themselves…

Since your community was born, the world has become "global": the economy and communications are, so to speak, "unified." But for many people, especially the poor, new walls have been built. Diversity is an opportunity for hostility and conflict; a *globalization of solidarity and of the Spirit* is yet to be built. The future of the global world is to live together; this ideal requires a commitment to build bridges, maintain open dialogue, and to continue to encounter one another.

It is not just a political or organizational issue. Each one is called to change his or her heart by turning *a merciful gaze* upon the other, by becoming an artisan of peace and a prophet of mercy. The Samaritan in the parable took care of the dying man on the road because he "saw and had compassion" (Lk 10:33). The Samaritan was a foreigner and had no specific responsibility toward the wounded man. Yet he behaved like a brother, because he had a merciful gaze. A Christian, by vocation, is the brother and sister of every person, especially if he or she is poor, even an enemy. Never say, "What do I have to do with him or her?" That is just a nice way of washing one's hands! "What have I to do with him?" A merciful gaze commits us to the creative boldness of love; there is so much need of it! We are everyone's brothers and sisters and, for this reason, prophets of a new world; and the Church is a sign of unity of the human race, among people, families, cultures.

I would like this anniversary to be a Christian anniversary: not a time to measure results or difficulties, not an hour for accounting, but a time when faith is called to become *newly bold for the Gospel*. Boldness is not one day's courage, but the patience of a daily mission in the city and in the world. The mission is to patiently mend the human fabric of the peripheries, which violence and impoverishment have torn apart; to communicate the Gospel through personal friendship; to show how a life becomes truly human when it is lived alongside the poorest; to create a society in which no one is a stranger any longer. The mission is to cross borders and transcend walls to reunite.

Today, may you continue ever more boldly along this path; continue to be close to the children of the peripheries with the Schools of Peace that I visited; continue to accompany the elderly: sometimes they are discarded, but to you they are friends; continue to open humanitarian corridors for refugees from war and hunger. The poor are your treasure!

The Apostle Paul writes: "Let no one boast of men, for all things are yours . . . and you are Christ's; and Christ is God's" (1 Cor 3:21, 23). You are Christ's! This is the profound meaning of your history to date, but it is above all the key to facing the future. Always be Christ's in prayer, in caring for the least of his brothers and sisters, searching for peace, because he is our peace. He will walk with you, protect you and guide you! I pray for you, and you pray for me. Thank you.

Ideologies Striking at the Heart of the Gospel

From the Apostolic Exhortation
Gaudate et Exsultate *(Nos. 100–103)*
March 19, 2018

I regret that ideologies lead us at times to two harmful errors. On the one hand, there is the error of those Christians who separate these gospel demands from their personal relationship with the Lord, from their interior union with him, from openness to his grace...

The other harmful ideological error is found in those who find suspect the social engagement of others, seeing it as superficial, worldly, secular, materialist, communist, or populist. Or they relativize it, as if there are other more important matters, or the only thing that counts is one particular ethical issue or cause that they themselves defend. Our defense of the innocent unborn, for example, needs to be clear, firm, and passionate, for at stake is the dignity of a human life, which is always sacred and demands love for each person, regardless of his or her stage of development. Equally sacred, however, are the lives of the poor, those already born, the destitute, the abandoned, and the underprivileged, the vulnerable infirm and elderly exposed to covert euthanasia, the victims of human trafficking, new forms of slavery, and every form of rejection. We cannot uphold an ideal of holiness that would ignore injustice in a world where some revel, spend with abandon, and live only for the latest consumer goods, even as others look on from afar, living their entire lives in abject poverty.

We often hear it said that, with respect to relativism and the flaws of our present world, the situation of migrants, for example, is a lesser issue. Some Catholics consider it a secondary issue compared to the "grave" bioethical questions. That a politician looking for votes might say such a thing is understandable, but not a Christian, for whom the only proper attitude is to stand in the shoes of those brothers and sisters of ours who risk their lives to offer a future to their children. Can we not realize that this is exactly what Jesus demands of us when he tells us that in welcoming the stranger we welcome him (cf. Mt 25:35)? Saint Benedict did so readily, and though it might have "complicated" the life of his monks, he ordered that all guests who knocked at the monastery door be welcomed "like Christ," with a gesture of veneration; the poor and pilgrims were to be met with "the greatest care and solicitude."

A similar approach is found in the Old Testament: "You shall not wrong a stranger or oppress him, for you yourselves were strangers in the land of Egypt" (Ex 22:21). "When a stranger resides with you in your land, you shall not oppress him. The stranger who resides with you shall be to you as the citizen among you; and you shall love him as yourself; for you were strangers in the land of Egypt" (Lev 19:33–34). This is not a notion invented by some pope, or a momentary fad. In today's world too, we are called to follow the path of spiritual wisdom proposed by the prophet Isaiah to show what is pleasing to God. "Is it not to share your bread with the hungry and bring the homeless poor into your house; when you see the naked, to cover him, and not to hide yourself from your own kin? Then your light shall break forth like the dawn" (58:7–8).

Migrants and Refugees

Men and Women in Search of Peace

Message for the Celebration of the Fifty-first World Day of Peace
January 1, 2018

1. Heartfelt good wishes for peace

Peace to all people and to all nations on earth! Peace, which the angels proclaimed to the shepherds on Christmas night,[1] is a profound aspiration for everyone, for each individual and all peoples, and especially for those who most keenly suffer its absence. Among these whom I constantly keep in my thoughts and prayers, I would once again mention the more than 250 million migrants worldwide, of whom 22.5 million are refugees. Pope Benedict XVI, my beloved predecessor, spoke of them as "men and women, children, young and elderly people, who are searching for somewhere to live in peace."[2] In order to find that peace, they are willing to risk their lives on a journey that is often long and perilous, to endure hardships and suffering, and to encounter fences and walls built to keep them far from their goal.

In a spirit of compassion, let us embrace all those fleeing from war and hunger, or forced by discrimination, persecution, poverty, and environmental degradation to leave their homelands. We know that it is not enough to open our hearts to the suffering of others. Much more remains to be done before our brothers and sisters can once again live peacefully in a safe home. Welcoming others requires concrete commitment, a network of assistance and goodwill, vigilant and sympathetic attention, the responsible management of new and complex situations that at times compound numerous existing problems, to say nothing of resources, which are always limited. By practicing the virtue of prudence, government leaders should take practical measures to welcome, promote, protect, integrate, and, "within the limits allowed by a correct understanding of the common good, to permit [them] to become part of a new society."[3] Leaders have a clear responsibility toward their own communities, whose legitimate rights and harmonious development they must ensure, lest they become like the rash builder who miscalculated and failed to complete the tower he had begun to construct.[4]

2. Why so many refugees and migrants?

As he looked to the Great Jubilee marking the passage of two thousand years since the proclamation of peace by the angels in Bethlehem, Saint John Paul II pointed to the increased numbers of displaced persons as one of the consequences of the "endless and horrifying sequence of wars, conflicts, genocides, and ethnic cleansings"[5] that had characterized the twentieth century. To this date, the new century has registered no real breakthrough: armed conflicts and other forms of organized violence continue to trigger the movement of peoples within national borders and beyond.

Yet people migrate for other reasons as well, principally because they "desire a better life, and not infrequently try to leave behind the 'hopelessness' of an unpromising future." [6] They set out to join their families or to seek professional or educational opportunities, for those who cannot enjoy these rights do not live in peace. Furthermore, as I noted in the encyclical *Laudato Si'*, there has been "a tragic rise in the number of migrants seeking to flee from the growing poverty caused by environmental degradation."[7]

Most people migrate through regular channels. Some, however, take different routes, mainly out of desperation, when their own countries offer neither safety nor opportunity and every legal pathway appears impractical, blocked, or too slow.

Many destination countries have seen the spread of rhetoric decrying the risks posed to national security or the high cost of welcoming new arrivals, and thus demeaning the human dignity due to all as sons and daughters of God. Those who, for what may be political reasons, foment fear of migrants instead of building peace are sowing violence, racial discrimination, and xenophobia, which are matters of great concern for all those concerned for the safety of every human being.[8]

All indicators available to the international community suggest that global migration will continue for the future. Some consider this a threat. For my part, I ask you to view it with confidence as an opportunity to build peace.

3. With a contemplative gaze
The wisdom of faith fosters a contemplative gaze that recognizes that all of us "belong to one family, migrants and the local populations that welcome them, and all have the same

right to enjoy the goods of the earth, whose destination is universal, as the social doctrine of the Church teaches. It is here that solidarity and sharing are founded."[9] These words evoke the biblical image of the new Jerusalem. The book of the prophet Isaiah (chapter 60) and that of Revelation (chapter 21) describe the city with its gates always open to people of every nation, who marvel at it and fill it with riches. Peace is the sovereign that guides it and justice the principle that governs coexistence within it.

We must also turn this contemplative gaze to the cities where we live, "a gaze of faith which sees God dwelling in their houses, in their streets and squares, . . . fostering solidarity, fraternity, and the desire for goodness, truth, and justice"[10] —in other words, fulfilling the promise of peace.

When we turn that gaze to migrants and refugees, we discover that they do not arrive empty-handed. They bring their courage, skills, energy, and aspirations, as well as the treasures of their own cultures; and in this way, they enrich the lives of the nations that receive them. We also come to see the creativity, tenacity, and spirit of sacrifice of the countless individuals, families, and communities around the world who open their doors and hearts to migrants and refugees, even where resources are scarce.

A contemplative gaze should also guide the discernment of those responsible for the public good, and encourage them to pursue policies of welcome "within the limits allowed by a correct understanding of the common good"[11]—bearing in mind, that is, the needs of all members of the human family and the welfare of each.

Those who see things in this way will be able to recognize the seeds of peace that are already sprouting and nurture their growth. Our cities, often divided and polarized by conflicts regarding the presence of migrants and refugees, will thus turn into workshops of peace.

4. *Four mileposts for action*

Offering asylum seekers, refugees, migrants and victims of human trafficking an opportunity to find the peace they seek requires a strategy combining four actions: welcoming, protecting, promoting, and integrating.[12]

"Welcoming" calls for expanding legal pathways for entry and no longer pushing migrants and displaced people toward countries where they face persecution and violence. It also demands balancing our concerns about national security with concern for fundamental human rights. Scripture reminds us: "Do not forget to show hospitality to strangers, for by so doing some people have shown hospitality to angels without knowing it."[13]

"Protecting" has to do with our duty to recognize and defend the inviolable dignity of those who flee real dangers in search of asylum and security, and to prevent their being exploited. I think in particular of women and children who find themselves in situations that expose them to risks and abuses that can even amount to enslavement. God does not discriminate: "The Lord watches over the foreigner and sustains the orphan and the widow."[14]

"Promoting" entails supporting the integral human development of migrants and refugees. Among many possible means of doing so, I would stress the importance of ensuring access to all levels of education for children and young people. This will not only enable them to cultivate and realize their potential but also better equip them to encounter others and to foster a spirit of dialogue rather than rejection or confrontation. The Bible teaches that God "loves the foreigner residing among you, giving them food and clothing. And you are to love those who are foreigners, for you yourselves were foreigners in Egypt."[15]

"Integrating," finally, means allowing refugees and migrants to participate fully in the life of the society that welcomes them, as part of a process of mutual enrichment and fruitful cooperation in service of the integral human development of the local community. St. Paul expresses it in these words: "You are no longer foreigners and strangers, but fellow citizens with God's people."[16]

5. A proposal for two international compacts

It is my heartfelt hope that this spirit will guide the process that in the course of 2018 will lead the United Nations to draft and approve two global compacts, one for safe, orderly, and regular migration and the other for refugees. As shared agreements at a global level, these compacts will provide a framework for policy proposals and practical measures. For this reason, they need to be inspired by compassion, foresight, and courage so as to take advantage of every opportunity to advance the peace-building process. Only in this way can the realism required of international politics avoid surrendering to cynicism and to the globalization of indifference.

Dialogue and coordination are a necessity and a specific duty for the international community. Beyond national borders, higher numbers of refugees may be welcomed—or better welcomed—also by less wealthy countries, if international cooperation guarantees them the necessary funding.

The Migrants and Refugees Section of the Dicastery for Promoting Integral Human Development has published a set of twenty action points that provide concrete leads for implementing these four verbs [to welcome, to protect, to promote, to integrate] in public policy and in the attitudes and activities of Christian communities.[17] The aim of this and other contributions is to express the interest of the Catholic Church in the process leading to the adoption of the two U.N. global compacts. This interest is the sign of a more general pastoral concern that goes back to the very origins of the Church and has continued in her many works up to the present time.

6. *For our common home*

Let us draw inspiration from the words of Saint John Paul II: "If the 'dream' of a peaceful world is shared by all, if the refugees' and migrants' contribution is properly evaluated, then humanity can become more and more a universal family and our earth a true 'common home.'"[18] Throughout history, many have believed in this "dream," and their achievements are a testament to the fact that it is no mere utopia.

Among these, we remember Saint Frances Xavier Cabrini in this year that marks the hundredth anniversary of her death. On this thirteenth day of November, many ecclesial communities celebrate her memory. This remarkable woman, who devoted her life to the service of migrants and became their patron saint, taught us to welcome, protect, promote, and integrate our brothers and sisters. Through her intercession, may the Lord enable all of us to experience that "a harvest of righteousness is sown in peace by those who make peace."[19]

From the Vatican, November 13, 2017
Memorial of Saint Frances Xavier Cabrini, Patroness of Migrants

Notes

1. Luke 2:14.

2. Angelus, January 15, 2012.

3. John XXIII, Encyclical Letter *Pacem in Terris*, 106.

4. Luke 14:28-30.

5. *Message for the 2000 World Day of Peace, 3.*.

6. Benedict XVI, *Message for the 2013 World Day of Migrants and Refugees*.

7. No. 25.

8. Cf. *Address to the National Directors of Pastoral Care for Migrants of the Catholic Bishops' Conferences of Europe*, September 22, 2017.

9. Benedict XVI, *Message for the 2011 World Day of Migrants and Refugees*.

10. Apostolic Exhortation *Evangelii Gaudium*, 71.

11. John XXIII, Encyclical Letter *Pacem in Terris*, 106.

12. *Message for the 2018 World Day of Migrants and Refugees.*

13. Hebrews 13:2.

14. Psalm 146:9.

15. Deuteronomy 10:18–19.

16. Ephesians 2:19.

17. "20 Pastoral Action Points" and "20 Action Points for the Global Compacts," Migrants and Refugees Section, Rome, 2017. See also Document UN A/72/528.

18. *Message for the World Day of Migrants and Refugees 2004, 6.*

19. James 3:18.

PART II

MESSAGES FOR THE WORLD DAY OF MIGRANTS AND REFUGEES

"Migrants and refugees are not pawns on the chessboard of humanity. They are children, women and men who leave or who are forced to leave their homes for various reasons, who share a legitimate desire for knowing and having, but above all for being more... A change of attitude toward migrants and refugees is needed on the part of everyone, moving away from attitudes of defensiveness and fear, indifference and marginalization—all typical of a throwaway culture—toward attitudes based on a culture of encounter, the only culture capable of building a better, more just and fraternal world."

—Message for 2014

Message for 2014

Migrants and Refugees:
Toward a Better World

Dear Brothers and Sisters,

Our societies are experiencing, in an unprecedented way, processes of mutual interdependence and interaction on the global level. While not lacking problematic or negative elements, these processes are aimed at improving the living conditions of the human family, not only economically but politically and culturally as well. Each individual is a part of humanity and, with the entire family of peoples, shares the hope of a better future. This consideration inspired the theme I have chosen for the World Day of Migrants and Refugees this year: *Migrants and Refugees: Toward a Better World.*

In our changing world, the growing phenomenon of human mobility emerges, to use the words of Pope Benedict XVI, as a "sign of the times" (cf. *Message for the 2006 World Day of Migrants and Refugees*). While it is true that migrations often reveal failures and shortcomings on the part of states and the international community, they also point to the aspiration of humanity to enjoy a unity marked by respect for differences, by attitudes of acceptance and hospitality which enable an equitable sharing of the world's goods, and by the protection and the advancement of the dignity and centrality of each human being.

From the Christian standpoint, the reality of migration, like other human realities, points to the tension between the beauty of creation, marked by grace and the redemption, and the mystery of sin. Solidarity, acceptance, and signs of fraternity and understanding exist side by side with rejection, discrimination, trafficking and exploitation, suffering and death. Particularly disturbing are those situations where migration is not only involuntary, but actually set in motion by various forms of human trafficking and enslavement. Nowadays, "slave labor" is common currency! Yet despite the problems, risks, and difficulties to be faced, great numbers of migrants and refugees continue to be inspired by confidence and hope; in their hearts they long for a better future, not only for themselves but for their families and those closest to them.

What is involved in the creation of "a better world"? The expression does not allude naively to abstract notions or unattainable ideals; rather, it aims at an authentic and integral development, at efforts to provide dignified living conditions for everyone, at finding just responses to the needs of individuals and families, and at ensuring that God's gift of creation is respected, safeguarded and cultivated. The Venerable Paul VI described the aspirations of people today in this way: "to secure a sure food supply, cures for diseases and steady employment . . . to exercise greater personal responsibility; to do more, to learn more, and have more, in order to be more" (*Populorum Progressio*, 6).

Our hearts do desire something "more." Beyond greater knowledge or possessions, they want to "be" more. Development cannot be reduced to economic growth alone, often attained without a thought for the poor and the vulnerable. A better world will come about only if attention is first paid to individuals; if human promotion is integral, taking account of every dimension of the person, including the spiritual; if no one is neglected, including the poor, the sick, prisoners, the needy and the stranger (cf. Mt 25:31–46); if we can prove capable of leaving behind a throwaway culture and embracing one of encounter and acceptance.

Migrants and refugees are not pawns on the chessboard of humanity. They are children, women and men who leave or who are forced to leave their homes for various reasons, who share a legitimate desire for knowing and having, but above all for being more. The sheer number of people migrating from one continent to another, or shifting places within their own countries and geographical areas, is striking. Contemporary movements of migration represent the largest movement of individuals, if not of peoples, in history. As the Church accompanies migrants and refugees on their journey, she seeks to understand the causes of migration, but she also works to overcome its negative effects and to maximize its positive influence on the communities of origin, transit, and destination.

While encouraging the development of a better world, we cannot remain silent about the scandal of poverty in its various forms. Violence, exploitation, discrimination, marginalization, restrictive approaches to fundamental freedoms, whether of individuals or of groups: these are some of the chief elements of poverty that need to be overcome. Often these are precisely the elements that mark migratory movements, thus linking migration to poverty. Fleeing from situations of extreme poverty or persecution in the hope of a better future, or simply to save their own lives, millions of persons choose to migrate. Despite their hopes and expectations, they often encounter mistrust, rejection, and exclusion, to say nothing of tragedies and disasters that batter their human dignity.

The reality of migration, given its new dimensions in our age of globalization, needs to be approached and managed in a new, equitable, and effective manner; more than anything, this calls for international cooperation and a spirit of profound solidarity and compassion. Cooperation at different levels is critical, and it includes the broad adoption of policies and rules aimed at protecting and promoting the human person. Pope Benedict XVI sketched the parameters of such policies, stating that they "should set out from close collaboration between the migrants' countries of origin and their countries of destination; they should be accompanied by adequate international norms able to coordinate different legislative systems with a view to safeguarding the needs and rights of individual migrants and their families, and at the same time, those of the host countries" (*Caritas in Veritate*, 62). Working together for a better world requires that countries help one another in a spirit of willingness and trust, without raising insurmountable barriers. A good synergy can be a source of encouragement to government leaders as they confront socioeconomic imbalances and an unregulated globalization, which are among some of the causes of migration movements in which individuals are more victims than protagonists. No country can singlehandedly face the difficulties associated with this phenomenon, which is now so widespread that it affects every continent in the twofold movement of immigration and emigration.

It must also be emphasized that such cooperation begins with the efforts of each country to create better economic and social conditions at home, so that emigration will not be the only option left for those who seek peace, justice, security, and full respect of their human dignity. The creation of opportunities for employment in the local economies will also help to avert the separation of families and ensure that individuals and groups enjoy conditions of stability and serenity.

Finally, in considering the situation of migrants and refugees, I would point to yet another element in building a better world, namely, the elimination of prejudices and presuppositions in the approach to migration. Not infrequently, the arrival of migrants, displaced persons, asylum-seekers, and refugees gives rise to suspicion and hostility. There is a fear that society will become less secure, that identity and culture will be lost, that competition for jobs will become stiffer, and even that criminal activity will increase. The communications media have a role of great responsibility in this regard; it is up to them, in fact, to break down stereotypes and to offer correct information in reporting the errors of a few as well as the honesty, rectitude, and goodness of the majority. A change of attitude toward migrants and refugees is needed on the part of everyone, moving away from attitudes of defensiveness and fear, indifference and marginalization—all typical of a throwaway culture—toward attitudes based on a culture of encounter, the only culture capable of building a better, more just and fraternal world. The communications media are themselves called to embrace this "conversion of attitudes" and to promote change in the way migrants and refugees are treated.

I think of how even the holy family of Nazareth experienced initial rejection: Mary "gave birth to her firstborn son, and wrapped him in swaddling clothes, and laid him in a manger, because there was no place for them in the inn" (Lk 2:7). Jesus, Mary, and Joseph knew what it meant to leave their own country and become migrants: threatened by Herod's lust for power, they were forced to take flight and seek refuge in Egypt (cf. Mt 2:13–14). But the maternal heart of Mary and the compassionate heart of Joseph, the protector of the holy family, never doubted that God would always be with them. Through their intercession, may that same firm certainty dwell in the heart of every migrant and refugee.

The Church, responding to Christ's command to "go and make disciples of all nations," is called to be the People of God that embraces all peoples and brings to them the proclamation of the Gospel, for the face of each person bears the mark of the face of Christ! Here we find the deepest foundation of the dignity of the human person, which must always be respected and safeguarded. It is less the criteria of efficiency, productivity, social class, or ethnic or religious belonging which ground that personal dignity so much as the fact of being created in God's own image and likeness (cf. Gen 1:26–27) and, even more so, being children of God. Every human being is a child of God! He or she bears the image of Christ! We ourselves need to see, and then to enable others to see, that migrants and refugees do not only represent a problem to be solved but are brothers and sisters to be welcomed, respected, and loved. They are an occasion that Providence gives us to help build a more just society, a more perfect democracy, a more united country, a more fraternal world, and a more open and evangelical Christian community. Migration can offer possibilities for a new evangelization and open vistas for the growth of a new humanity foreshadowed in the paschal mystery: a humanity for which every foreign country is a homeland and every homeland is a foreign country.

Dear migrants and refugees! Never lose the hope that you too are facing a more secure future, that on your journey you will encounter an outstretched hand, and that you can experience fraternal solidarity and the warmth of friendship! To all of you, and to those who have devoted their lives and their efforts to helping you, I give the assurance of my prayers and I cordially impart my Apostolic Blessing.

—*From the Vatican, August 5, 2013*

Message for 2015

Church without Frontiers, Mother to All

Dear Brothers and Sisters,

Jesus is "the evangelizer par excellence and the Gospel in person" (*Evangelii Gaudium*, 209). His solicitude, particularly for the most vulnerable and marginalized, invites all of us to care for the frailest and to recognize his suffering countenance, especially in the victims of new forms of poverty and slavery. The Lord says: "I was hungry and you gave me food, I was thirsty and you gave me drink, I was a stranger and you welcomed me, I was naked and you clothed me, I was sick and you visited me, I was in prison and you came to me" (Mt 25:35–36). The mission of the Church, herself a pilgrim in the world and the Mother of all, is thus to love Jesus Christ, to adore and love him, particularly in the poorest and most abandoned; among these are certainly migrants and refugees, who are trying to escape difficult living conditions and dangers of every kind. For this reason, the theme for this year's World Day of Migrants and Refugees is: *Church without frontiers, Mother to all*.

The Church opens her arms to welcome all people, without distinction or limits, in order to proclaim that "God is love" (1 Jn 4:8, 16). After his death and resurrection, Jesus entrusted to the disciples the mission of being his witnesses and proclaiming the Gospel of joy and mercy. On the day of Pentecost, the disciples left the Upper Room with courage and enthusiasm; the strength of the Holy Spirit overcame their doubts and uncertainties and enabled all to understand the disciples' preaching in their own language. From the beginning, the Church has been a mother with a heart open to the whole world, and has been without borders. This mission has continued for two thousand years. But even in the first centuries, the missionary proclamation spoke of the universal motherhood of the Church, which was then developed in the writings of the Fathers and taken up by the Second Vatican Council. The Council Fathers spoke of *Ecclesia Mater* to explain the Church's nature. She begets sons and daughters and "takes them in and embraces them with her love and in her heart" (*Lumen Gentium*, 14).

The Church without frontiers, Mother to all, spreads throughout the world a culture of acceptance and solidarity, in which no one is seen as useless, out of place, or disposable. When living out this motherhood effectively, the Christian community nourishes, guides, and shows the way, accompanying all with patience, and drawing close to all through prayer and works of mercy.

Today this takes on a particular significance. In fact, in an age of such vast movements of migration, large numbers of people are leaving their homelands, with a suitcase full of fears and desires, to undertake a hopeful and dangerous trip in search of more humane living conditions. Often, however, such migration gives rise to suspicion and hostility, even in ecclesial communities, prior to any knowledge of the migrants' lives or their stories of persecution and destitution. In such cases, suspicion and prejudice conflict with the biblical commandment of welcoming with respect and solidarity the stranger in need.

On the other hand, we sense in our conscience the call to touch human misery and to put into practice the commandment of love that Jesus left us when he identified himself with the stranger, with the one who suffers, with all the innocent victims of violence and exploitation. Because of the weakness of our nature, however, "we are tempted to be that kind of Christian who keeps the Lord's wounds at arm's length" (*Evangelii Gaudium*, 270).

The courage born of faith, hope, and love enables us to reduce the distances that separate us from human misery. Jesus Christ is always waiting to be recognized in migrants and refugees, in displaced persons, and in exiles, and through them he calls us to share our resources and occasionally to give up something of our acquired riches. Pope Paul VI spoke of this when he said that "the more fortunate should renounce some of their rights so as to place their goods more generously at the service of others" (*Octogesima Adveniens*, 23).

The multicultural character of society today, for that matter, encourages the Church to take on new commitments of solidarity, communion, and evangelization. Migration movements, in fact, call us to deepen and strengthen the values needed to guarantee peaceful coexistence between persons and cultures. Achieving mere tolerance that respects diversity and ways of sharing between different backgrounds and cultures is not sufficient. This is precisely where the Church contributes to overcoming frontiers and encouraging the "moving away from attitudes of defensiveness and fear, indifference and marginalization ... toward attitudes based on a culture of encounter, the only culture capable of building a better, more just and fraternal world" (*Message for the World Day of Migrants and Refugees 2014*).

Migration movements, however, are on such a scale that only a systematic and active cooperation between states and international organizations can be capable of regulating and managing such movements effectively, for migration affects everyone, not only because of the extent of the phenomenon but also because of "the social, economic, political, cultural, and religious problems it raises, and the dramatic challenges it poses to nations and the international community" (*Caritas in Veritate*, 62).

At the international level, frequent debates take place regarding the appropriateness, methods, and required norms to deal with the phenomenon of migration. There are agencies and organizations on the international, national, and local level that work strenuously to serve those seeking a better life through migration. Notwithstanding their generous and laudable efforts, a more decisive and constructive action is required, one that relies on a universal network of cooperation based on safeguarding the dignity and centrality of every human person. This will lead to greater effectiveness in the fight against the shameful and criminal trafficking of human beings, the violation of fundamental rights, and all forms of violence, oppression, and enslavement. Working together, however, requires reciprocity, joint action, openness, and trust, in the knowledge that "no country can singlehandedly face the difficulties associated with this phenomenon, which is now so widespread that it affects every continent in the twofold movement of immigration and emigration" (*Message for the World Day of Migrants and Refugees 2014*).

It is necessary to respond to the globalization of migration with the globalization of charity and cooperation in such a way as to make the conditions of migrants more humane. At the same time, greater efforts are needed to guarantee the easing of conditions, often brought about by war or famine, that compel whole peoples to leave their native countries.

Solidarity with migrants and refugees must be accompanied by the courage and creativity necessary to develop, on a worldwide level, a more just and equitable financial and economic order, as well as an increasing commitment to peace, the indispensable condition for all authentic progress.

Dear migrants and refugees! You have a special place in the heart of the Church, and you help her to enlarge her heart and to manifest her motherhood toward the entire human family. Do not lose your faith and hope! Let us think of the holy family during the flight in Egypt: just as the maternal heart of the Blessed Virgin and the kind heart of Saint Joseph kept alive the confidence that God would never abandon them, so in you may the same hope in the Lord never be wanting. I entrust you to their protection and I cordially impart to all of you my Apostolic Blessing.

—*From the Vatican, September 3, 2014*

Message for 2016

Migrants and Refugees Challenge Us:
The Response of the Gospel of Mercy

Dear Brothers and Sisters,

In the Bull of Indiction [formal papal document] announcing the Extraordinary Jubilee of Mercy I noted that "at times we are called to gaze even more attentively on mercy so that we may become a more effective sign of the Father's action in our lives" (*Misericordiae Vultus*, 3). God's love is meant to reach out to each and every person. Those who welcome the Father's embrace, for their part, become so many other open arms and embraces, enabling every person to feel loved like a child and "at home" as part of the one human family. God's fatherly care extends to everyone, like the care of a shepherd for his flock, but it is particularly concerned for the needs of the sheep who are wounded, weary, or ill. Jesus told us that the Father stoops to help those overcome by physical or moral poverty; the more serious their condition, the more powerfully is his divine mercy revealed.

In our time, migration is growing worldwide. Refugees and people fleeing from their homes challenge individuals and communities and their traditional ways of life; at times

they upset the cultural and social horizons that they encounter. Increasingly, victims of violence and poverty, leaving their homelands, are exploited by human traffickers
during their journey toward the dream of a better future. If
they survive the abuses and hardships of the journey, they
then have to face latent suspicions and fear. In the end, they
frequently encounter a dearth of clear and practical policies
regulating the acceptance of migrants and providing for
short- or long-term programs of integration respectful of the
rights and duties of all. Today, more than in the past, the
Gospel of mercy troubles our consciences, prevents us from
taking the suffering of others for granted, and points out
ways of responding which, grounded in the theological
virtues of faith, hope and charity, find practical expression in
works of spiritual and corporal mercy.

In the light of these facts, I have chosen as the theme of
the 2016 World Day of Migrants and Refugees *Migrants and
Refugees Challenge Us: The Response of the Gospel of Mercy*. Migration movements are now a structural reality, and our primary issue must be to deal with the present emergency phase
by providing programs that address the causes of migration
and the changes it entails, including its effects on the makeup
of societies and peoples. The tragic stories of millions of men
and women daily confront the international community as a
result of the outbreak of unacceptable humanitarian crises in
different parts of the world. Indifference and silence lead to
complicity whenever we stand by as people are dying of suf-
focation, starvation, violence, and shipwreck. Whether large
or small in scale, these are always tragedies, even when a single human life is lost.

Migrants are our brothers and sisters in search of a better
life, far away from poverty, hunger, exploitation, and the un-

just distribution of the planet's resources, which are meant to be equitably shared by all. Don't we all want a better, more decent and prosperous life to share with our loved ones?

At this moment in human history, marked by great movements of migration, identity is not a secondary issue. Those who migrate are forced to change some of their most distinctive characteristics and, whether they like it or not, even those who welcome them are also forced to change. How can we experience these changes not as obstacles to genuine development but rather as opportunities for genuine human, social, and spiritual growth, a growth that respects and promotes those values that make us ever more humane and help us to live a balanced relationship with God, others, and creation?

The presence of migrants and refugees seriously challenges the various societies that accept them. Those societies are faced with new situations that could create serious hardship unless they are suitably motivated, managed, and regulated. How can we ensure that integration will become mutual enrichment, open up positive perspectives to communities, and prevent the danger of discrimination, racism, extreme nationalism, or xenophobia?

Biblical revelation urges us to welcome the stranger; it tells us that in so doing we open our doors to God, and that in the faces of others we see the face of Christ himself. Many institutions, associations, movements and groups, diocesan, national, and international organizations are experiencing the wonder and joy of the feast of encounter, sharing, and solidarity. They have heard the voice of Jesus Christ: "Behold, I stand at the door and knock" (Rev 3:20). Yet there continue to be debates about the conditions and limits to be set for the reception of migrants, not only on the level of national

policies but also in some parish communities whose traditional tranquility seems to be threatened.

Faced with these issues, how can the Church fail to be inspired by the example and words of Jesus Christ? The answer of the Gospel is mercy.

In the first place, mercy is a gift of God the Father who is
revealed in the Son. God's mercy gives rise to joyful gratitude for the hope that opens up before us in the mystery of
our redemption by Christ's blood. Mercy nourishes and
strengthens solidarity toward others as a necessary response
to God's gracious love, "which has been poured into our
hearts through the Holy Spirit" (Rom 5:5). Each of us is responsible for his or her neighbor: we are our brothers' and
sisters' keepers, wherever they live. Concern for fostering
good relationships with others and the ability to overcome
prejudice and fear are essential ingredients for promoting the
culture of encounter in which we are prepared not only to
give but also to receive from others. Hospitality, in fact,
grows from both giving and receiving.

From this perspective, it is important to view migrants
not only on the basis of their status as regular or irregular but
above all as people whose dignity is to be protected and who
are capable of contributing to progress and the general welfare. This is especially the case when they responsibly assume their obligations toward those who receive them,
gratefully respecting the material and spiritual heritage of
the host country, obeying its laws and helping with its needs.
Migrations cannot be reduced merely to their political and
legislative aspects, their economic implications, and the concrete coexistence of various cultures in one territory. All these
complement the defense and promotion of the human person, the culture of encounter, and the unity of peoples, where

the Gospel of mercy inspires and encourages ways of renewing and transforming the whole of humanity.

The Church stands at the side of all who work to defend each person's right to live with dignity, first and foremost by exercising the right not to emigrate and to contribute to the development of one's country of origin. This process should include, from the outset, the necessity of assisting the countries that migrants and refugees have left. This will demonstrate that solidarity, cooperation, international interdependence, and the equitable distribution of the earth's goods are essential for more decisive efforts, especially in areas where migration movements begin, to eliminate those imbalances that lead people, individually or collectively, to abandon their own natural and cultural environment. In any case, it is necessary to avert, if possible at the earliest stages, the flight of refugees and departures as a result of poverty, violence, and persecution.

Public opinion also needs to be correctly formed, not least to prevent unwarranted fears and speculations detrimental to migrants.

No one can claim to be indifferent in the face of new forms of slavery imposed by criminal organizations that buy and sell men, women, and children as forced laborers in construction, agriculture, fishing, or other markets. How many minors are still forced to fight in militias as child soldiers! How many people are victims of organ trafficking, forced begging, and sexual exploitation! Today's refugees are fleeing from these aberrant crimes, and they appeal to the Church and the human community to ensure that, in the outstretched hand of those who receive them, they can see the face of the Lord, "the Father of mercies and God of all consolation" (2 Cor 1:3).

Dear brothers and sisters, migrants and refugees! At the heart of the Gospel of mercy the encounter and acceptance by others are intertwined with the encounter and acceptance of God himself. Welcoming others means welcoming God in person! Do not let yourselves be robbed of the hope and joy of life born of your experience of God's mercy as manifested in the people you meet on your journey! I entrust you to the Virgin Mary, Mother of migrants and refugees, and to Saint Joseph, who experienced the bitterness of emigration to Egypt. To their intercession I also commend those who invest so much energy and time and so many resources to the pastoral and social care of migrants. To all I cordially impart my Apostolic Blessing.

—*From the Vatican, September 12, 2015, Memorial of the Holy Name of Mary*

Message for 2017

Child Migrants, the Vulnerable, and the Voiceless

Dear Brothers and Sisters,

"Whoever receives one such child in my name receives me; and whoever receives me, receives not me but him who sent me" (Mk 9:37; cf. Mt 18:5; Lk 9:48; Jn 13:20). With these words, the evangelists remind the Christian community of Jesus' teaching, which both inspires and challenges. This phrase traces the sure path that leads to God; it begins with the smallest and, through the grace of our Savior, it grows into the practice of welcoming others. To be welcoming is a necessary condition for making this journey a concrete reality: God made himself one of us. In Jesus God became a child, and the openness of faith to God, which nourishes hope, is expressed in loving proximity to the smallest and the weakest. Charity, faith, and hope are all actively present in the spiritual and corporal works of mercy, as we have rediscovered during the recent Extraordinary Jubilee.

But the evangelists reflect also on the responsibility of the one who works against mercy: "Whoever causes one of these little ones who believe in me to sin, it is better for him to have a great millstone fastened round his neck and be drowned in the depth of the sea" (Mt 18:6; cf. Mk 9:42; Lk 17:2). How can we ignore this severe warning when we see the exploitation carried out by unscrupulous people? Such exploitation harms young girls and boys who are led into prostitution or into the mire of pornography; who are enslaved as child laborers or soldiers; who are caught up in drug trafficking and other forms of criminality; who are forced to flee from conflict and persecution, risking isolation and abandonment.

For this reason, on the occasion of the annual World Day of Migrants and Refugees, I feel compelled to draw attention to the reality of child migrants, especially the ones who are alone. In doing so I ask everyone to take care of the young, who in a threefold way are defenseless: they are children, they are foreigners, and they have no means to protect themselves. I ask everyone to help those who, for various reasons, are forced to live far from their homeland and are separated from their families.

Migration today is not a phenomenon limited to some areas of the planet. It affects all continents and is growing into a tragic situation of global proportions. Not only does this concern those looking for dignified work or better living conditions, but also men and women, the elderly and children, who are forced to leave their homes in the hope of finding safety, peace and security. Children are the first among those to pay the heavy toll of emigration, almost always caused by violence, poverty, environmental conditions, as well as the negative aspects of globalization. The unrestrained competition for quick and easy profit brings with it the cultivation of perverse scourges such as child trafficking, the exploitation and abuse of minors and, generally, the depriving of rights intrinsic to childhood as sanctioned by the International Convention on the Rights of the Child.

Childhood, given its fragile nature, has unique and innate needs. Above all else, there is the right to a healthy and secure family environment, where a child can grow under the guidance and example of a father and a mother; then there is the right and duty to receive adequate education, primarily in the family and also in school, where children can grow as persons and agents of their own future and the future of their respective countries. Indeed, in many areas of the world, reading, writing, and the most basic arithmetic is still the privilege of only a few. All children, furthermore, have the right to recreation; in a word, they have the right to be children.

And yet among migrants, children constitute the most vulnerable group, because as they face the life ahead of them they are invisible and voiceless: their precarious situation deprives them of documentation, hiding them from the world's eyes; the absence of adults to accompany them prevents their voices from being raised and heard. In this way, migrant children easily end up at the lowest levels of human degradation, where illegality and violence destroy the future of too many innocents, while the network of child abuse is difficult to break up.

How should we respond to this reality?

First, we need to become aware that the phenomenon of migration is not unrelated to salvation history, but rather is a part of that history. One of God's commandments is connected to it: "You shall not wrong a stranger or oppress him, for you were strangers in the land of Egypt" (Ex 22:21); "Love the sojourner therefore; for you were sojourners in the land of Egypt" (Deut 10:19). This phenomenon constitutes *a sign of the times*, a sign that speaks of the providential work of God in history and in the human community, with a view to universal communion. While appreciating the issues, and often the suffering and tragedy of migration as well as the difficulties connected with the demands of offering a dignified welcome to these persons, the Church nevertheless encourages us to recognize God's plan. She invites us to do this precisely amidst this phenomenon, with the certainty that no one is a stranger in the Christian community, which embraces "every nation, tribe, people and tongue" (Rev 7:9). Each person is precious; persons are more important than things, and the worth of an institution is measured by the way it treats the life and dignity of human beings, particularly when they are vulnerable, as in the case of child migrants.

Furthermore, we need to work toward *protection, integration,* and *long-term solutions.*

We are primarily concerned with adopting every possible measure to guarantee the *protection and safety* of child migrants, because "these boys and girls often end up on the street abandoned to themselves and prey to unscrupulous exploiters who often transform them into the object of physical, moral, and sexual violence" (Benedict XVI, *Message for the World Day of Migrants and Refugees,* 2008).

Moreover, the dividing line between migration and trafficking can at times be very subtle. There are many factors that contribute to making migrants vulnerable, especially if they are children: poverty and the lack of means to survive—to which are added unrealistic expectations generated by the media; the low level of literacy; ignorance of the law, of the culture, and frequently of the language of host countries. All of this renders children physically and psychologically dependent. But the most powerful force driving the exploitation and abuse of children is demand. If more rigorous and effective action is not taken against those who profit from such abuse, we will not be able to stop the multiple forms of slavery where children are the victims.

It is necessary, therefore, for immigrants to cooperate ever more closely with the communities that welcome them, for the good of their own children. We are deeply grateful to organizations and institutions, both ecclesial and civil, that commit time and resources to protecting minors from various forms of abuse. It is important that ever more effective and incisive cooperation be implemented, based not only on the exchange of information but also on the reinforcement of networks capable of assuring timely and specific intervention; and this without underestimating the strength that ecclesial communities reveal, especially when they are united in prayer and fraternal communion.

Second, we need to work for the *integration* of children and youngsters who are migrants. They depend totally on the adult community. Very often the scarcity of financial resources prevents the adoption of adequate policies aimed at assistance and inclusion. As a result, instead of favoring the social integration of child migrants or programs for safe and assisted repatriation, there is simply an attempt to curb the entrance of migrants, which in turn fosters illegal networks; or else immigrants are repatriated to their country of origin without any concern for their "best interests."

The condition of child migrants is worsened when their status is not regularized or when they are recruited by criminal organizations. In such cases they are usually sent to detention centers. It is not unusual for them to be arrested, and because they have no money to pay the fine or for the return journey, they can be incarcerated for long periods, exposed to various kinds of abuse and violence. In these instances, the right of states to control migratory movement and to protect the common good of the nation must be seen in conjunction with the duty to resolve and regularize the situation of child migrants, fully respecting their dignity and seeking to meet their needs when they are alone, but also the needs of their parents, for the good of the entire family.

Of fundamental importance is the adoption of adequate national procedures and mutually agreed plans of cooperation between countries of origin and of destination, with the intention of eliminating the causes of the forced emigration of minors.

Third, to all I address a heartfelt appeal that *long-term solutions* be sought and adopted. Since this is a complex phenomenon, the issue of child migrants must be tackled at its source. Wars, human rights violations, corruption, poverty, environmental imbalance, and disasters are all causes of this problem. Children are the first to suffer, at times suffering torture and other physical violence in addition to moral and psychological aggression, which almost always leave indelible scars.

It is absolutely necessary, therefore, to deal with the causes that trigger migrations in the countries of origin. This requires, as a first step, the commitment of the whole international community to eliminating the conflicts and violence that force people to flee. Furthermore, far-sighted perspectives are called for, capable of offering adequate programs for areas struck by the worst injustice and instability, in order that access to authentic development can be guaranteed for all. This development should promote the good of boys and girls, who are humanity's hope.

Finally, I wish to address a word to you who walk alongside migrant children and young people: they need your precious help. The Church too needs you and supports you in the generous service you offer. Do not tire of courageously living the Gospel, which calls you to recognize and welcome the Lord Jesus among the smallest and most vulnerable.

I entrust all child migrants, their families, their communities, and you who are close to them, to the protection of the Holy Family of Nazareth; may they watch over and accompany each one on their journey. With my prayers, I gladly impart my Apostolic Blessing.

—From the Vatican, September 8, 2016

Message for 2018

Welcoming, Protecting, Promoting, and Integrating Migrants and Refugees

Dear Brothers and Sisters!

"You shall treat the stranger who sojourns with you as the native among you, and you shall love him as yourself, for you were strangers in the land of Egypt: I am the Lord your God" (Lev 19:34).

Throughout the first years of my pontificate, I have repeatedly expressed my particular concern for the lamentable situation of many migrants and refugees fleeing from war, persecution, natural disasters, and poverty. This situation is undoubtedly a "sign of the times," which, with the help of the Holy Spirit, I have tried to interpret ever since my visit to Lampedusa on July 8, 2013. When I instituted the new Dicastery for Promoting Integral Human Development, I wanted a particular section—under my personal direction for the time being—to express the Church's concern for migrants, displaced people, refugees, and victims of human trafficking.

Every stranger who knocks at our door presents us with an opportunity for an encounter with Jesus Christ, who identifies with the welcomed and rejected strangers of every age

(Mt 25:35–43). The Lord entrusts to the Church's motherly love every person forced to leave his or her homeland in search of a better future.[1] This solidarity must be concretely expressed at every stage of the migratory experience—from departure through journey to arrival and return. This is a great responsibility, which the Church intends to share with all believers and men and women of good will, who are called to respond to the many challenges of contemporary migration with generosity, promptness, wisdom, and fore-sight, each according to his or her own abilities.

In this regard, I wish to reaffirm that "our shared response may be articulated by four verbs: *to welcome, to protect, to promote,* and *to integrate*."[2]

To welcome

Considering the current situation, *welcoming* means, above all, offering broader options for migrants and refugees to enter destination countries safely and legally. This calls for a concrete commitment to increase and simplify the process for granting humanitarian visas and for reunifying families. At the same time, I hope that a greater number of countries will adopt private and community sponsorship programs and open humanitarian corridors for particularly vulnerable refugees. Furthermore, special temporary visas should be granted to people fleeing conflicts in neighboring countries. Collective and arbitrary expulsions of migrants and refugees are not suitable solutions, particularly in cases where people are returned to countries that cannot guarantee respect for human dignity and fundamental rights.[3] Once again, I want to emphasize the importance of offering migrants and refugees adequate and dignified initial accommodation. "More widespread programs of welcome, already initiated in different places, seem to favor a personal encounter and allow for greater quality of service and increased guarantees of success."[4] The principle of the centrality of the human person, firmly stated by my beloved predecessor, Benedict XVI,[5] obliges us to always prioritize personal safety over national security. It is necessary, therefore, to ensure that agents in charge of border control are properly trained. The situation of migrants, asylum seekers, and refugees requires that they be guaranteed personal safety and access to basic services. For the sake of the fundamental dignity of every human person, we must strive to find alternative solutions to detention for those who enter a country without authorization.[6]

To protect

The second verb—*protecting*—may be understood as a series of steps intended to defend the rights and dignity of migrants and refugees, independent of their legal status.[7] Such protection begins in the country of origin and consists in offering reliable and verified information before departure and in providing safety from illegal recruitment practices.[8] This must be ongoing, as far as possible, in the country of arrival, guaranteeing them adequate consular assistance, the right to personally retain their identity documents at all times, fair access to justice, the possibility of opening a personal bank account, and a minimum of funds sufficient to live on. When duly recognized and valued, the potential and skills of migrants, asylum seekers, and refugees are a true resource for the communities that welcome them.[9] This is why I hope that, in countries of arrival, migrants may be offered, out of respect for their dignity, freedom of movement, work opportunities, and access to means of communication. For those who decide to return to their homeland, I want to emphasize the need to develop social and professional reintegration programs. The *International Convention on the Rights of the Child* provides a universal legal basis for the protection of underage migrants. They must be spared any form of detention related to migratory status and must be guaranteed regular access to primary and secondary education. Likewise, when they come of age they must be guaranteed the right to remain and to enjoy the possibility of continuing their studies. Temporary custody or foster programs should be provided for unaccompanied minors and minors separated from their families.[10] The universal right to a nationality should be recognized and duly certified for all children at birth. The statelessness that migrants and refugees sometimes fall into can easily be avoided with the adoption of "nationality legislation that is in conformity with the fundamental principles of international law."[11] Migratory status should not limit access to national healthcare and pension plans, nor affect the transfer of their contributions if repatriated.

To promote

Promoting essentially means undertaking a determined effort to ensure that all migrants and refugees—as well as the communities that welcome them—are empowered to achieve their potential as human beings in all the dimensions that constitute the humanity intended by the Creator.[12] Among these, we must recognize the true value of the religious dimension, ensuring to all foreigners in any country the freedom of religious belief and practice. Many migrants and refugees have abilities that must be appropriately recognized and valued. Since "work, by its nature, is meant to unite peoples,"[13] I encourage a determined effort to promote the social and professional inclusion of migrants and refugees, guaranteeing for all—including those seeking asylum—the possibility of employment, language instruction, and active citizenship, together with sufficient information provided in their mother tongue. In the case of underage migrants, their involvement in labor must be regulated to prevent exploitation and risks to their normal growth and development. In 2006, Benedict XVI highlighted how, in the context of migration, the family is "a place and resource of the culture of life and a factor for the integration of values."[14] The family's integrity must always be promoted, supporting family reunifications—including grandparents, grandchildren and siblings—independent of financial requirements. Migrants, asylum seekers, and refugees with disabilities must be granted greater assistance and support. While I recognize the praiseworthy efforts, thus far, of many countries, in terms of international cooperation and humanitarian aid, I hope that the offering of this assistance will take into account the needs (such as in the areas of medical and social assistance, as well as education) of developing countries that receive a significant influx of migrants and refugees. I also hope that local communities which are vulnerable and facing material hardship, will be included among aid beneficiaries.[15]

To integrate

The final verb—*integrating*—concerns the opportunities for intercultural enrichment brought about by the presence of migrants and refugees. Integration is not "an assimilation that leads migrants to suppress or to forget their own cultural identity. Rather, contact with others leads to discovering their 'secret,' to being open to them in order to welcome them and thus contribute to knowing each one better. This is a lengthy process that aims to shape societies and cultures, making them more and more a reflection of the multi-faceted gifts of God to human beings."[16] This process can be accelerated by granting citizenship free of financial or linguistic requirements, and by offering the possibility of special legalization to migrants who can claim a long period of residence in the country of arrival. I reiterate the need to foster a culture of encounter in every way possible—by increasing opportunities for intercultural exchange, documenting and disseminating best practices of integration, and developing programs to prepare local communities for integration processes. I wish to stress the special case of people forced to abandon their country of arrival because of a humanitarian crisis. These people must be ensured adequate assistance for repatriation and effective reintegration programs in their home countries.

In line with her pastoral tradition, the Church is ready to commit herself to realizing all the initiatives proposed above. Yet in order to achieve the desired outcome, the contribution of political communities and civil societies is indispensable, each according to its own responsibilities.

At the United Nations Summit held in New York on September 19, 2016, world leaders clearly expressed their desire to take decisive action in support of migrants and refugees to save their lives and protect their rights, sharing this responsibility on a global level. To this end, the states committed themselves to drafting and approving, before the end of 2018, two global compacts, one for refugees and the other for migrants.

Dear brothers and sisters, in light of these processes currently under way, the coming months offer a unique opportunity to advocate for and support the concrete actions that I have described with four verbs. I invite you, therefore, to use every occasion to share this message with all political and social actors who are involved (or who seek to be involved) in the process that will lead to the approval of the two global compacts.

Today, August 15, we celebrate the Feast of the Assumption of Mary. The Holy Mother of God herself experienced the hardship of exile (Mt 2:13–15), lovingly accompanied her son's journey to Calvary, and now shares eternally his glory. To her maternal intercession we entrust the hopes of all the world's migrants and refugees and the aspirations of the communities that welcome them, so that, responding to the Lord's supreme commandment, we may all learn to love the other, the stranger, as ourselves.

—*Vatican City, August 15, 2017*
Solemnity of the Assumption of the Blessed Virgin Mary

Notes

1. Cf. Pius XII, Apostolic Constitution *Exsul Familia, Titulus Primus,* I.

2. *Address to Participants in the International Forum on "Migration and Peace,"* February 21, 2017.

3. Cf. *Statement of the Permanent Observer of the Holy See to the 103rd Session of the Council of the IOM,* November 26, 2013.

4. *Address to Participants in the International Forum on "Migration and Peace,"* February 21, 2017.

5. Cf. Benedict XVI, Encyclical Letter *Caritas in Veritate,* 47.

6. Cf. *Statement of the Permanent Observer of the Holy See to the Twentieth Session of the UN Human Rights Council,* June 22, 2012.

7. Cf. Benedict XVI, Encyclical Letter *Caritas in Veritate,* 62.

8. Cf. Pontifical Council for the Pastoral Care of Migrants and Itinerant People, Instruction *Erga Migrantes Caritas Christi,* 6.

9. Cf. Benedict XVI, *Address to the Participants in the Sixth World Congress for the Pastoral Care of Migrants and Itinerant People,* November 9, 2009.

10. Cf. Benedict XVI, *Message for the World Day of Migrants and Refugees (2010)* and *Statement of the Permanent Observer of the Holy See to the Twenty-sixth Ordinary Session of the Human Rights Council on the Human Rights of Migrants*, June 13, 2014.

11. Pontifical Council for the Pastoral Care of Migrants and Itinerant People and Pontifical Council, *Cor Unum, Welcoming Christ in Refugees and Forcibly Displaced Persons*, 2013, 70.

12. Cf. Paul VI, Encyclical Letter *Populorum Progressio*, 14.

13. John Paul II, Encyclical Letter *Centesimus Annus*, 27.

14. Benedict XVI, *Message for the World Day of Migrants and Refugees* (2007).

15. Cf. Pontifical Council for the Pastoral Care of Migrants and Itinerant People and Pontifical Council, *Cor Unum, Welcoming Christ in Refugees and Forcibly Displaced Persons*, 2013, 30–31.

16. John Paul II, *Message for the World Day of Migrants and Refugees* (2005).

Final Words

From a Message for the
Second Holy See–Mexico Conference on International Migration
June 14, 2018

We must move from considering others as threats to our comfort to valuing them as persons whose life experience and values can contribute greatly to the enrichment of our society. For this to happen, our basic approach must be "to encounter the other, to welcome, to know, and to acknowledge him or her" (*Homily for the World Day of Migrants and Refugees*, January 14, 2018)...

The issue of migration is not simply one of *numbers* but of *persons*, each with his or her own history, culture, feelings, and aspirations...These persons, our brothers and sisters, need ongoing protection, independently of whatever migrant status they may have. Their fundamental rights and their dignity need to be protected and defended. Particular concern must be shown for migrant children and their families, those who are victims of human trafficking rings, and those displaced due to conflicts, natural disasters, and persecution. All of them hope that we will have the courage to tear down the wall of "comfortable and silent complicity" that worsens their helplessness; they are waiting for us to show them concern, compassion, and devotion.